A
PORTRAIT
of JESUS

A
PORTRAIT
of JESUS

JOSEPH F. GIRZONE

DOUBLEDAY

New York   London   Toronto   Sydney   Auckland

PUBLISHED BY DOUBLEDAY
a division of Bantam Doubleday Dell Publishing Group, Inc.
1540 Broadway, New York, New York 10036

DOUBLEDAY and the portrayal of an anchor with a dolphin are trademarks of Doubleday,
a division of Bantam Doubleday Dell Publishing Group, Inc.

Library of Congress Cataloging-in-Publication Data
Girzone, Joseph F.
A portrait of Jesus / Joseph F. Girzone. — 1st ed.
p.   cm.
1. Jesus Christ—Biography—Devotional literature.
2. Christian life—Catholic authors.   I. Title.
BT306.5.G75   1998
232.9'01
[B]—DC21   98-15618
CIP

Book design by Leah S. Carlson

Book illustrations by Stefano Vitale

ISBN 0-385-48263-9

Printed in the United States of America

October 1998

First Edition

1   3   5   7   9   10   8   6   4   2

I dedicate this book to Jesus
with the humble realization that others,
with more extensive training and greater talent,
could have given Him considerable more honor
than I have in this simple presentation.
My only hope is that those who read it
may be drawn into a deeper understanding of
Jesus and feel more comfortable in His love.

ACKNOWLEDGMENTS

I AM DEEPLY GRATEFUL to my publishers at Bantam Double-day Dell, and particularly to their sales force, whom I consider most valuable partners in my work of bringing these important messages to the reading public. May they be blessed. I am particularly grateful to Eric Major, the publisher, for his sensitive monitoring of each phase in the development of the manuscript, and especially my good and dear friend Trace Murphy, who works so patiently with me as we give birth to each new book.

I do not know how to thank my agent, Peter Ginsberg. He is not just a superb expert in his field. He is also a dear friend. I could never adequately thank him for all his help through the years. May he be richly blessed for having introduced to the world Joshua, and all the messages that followed.

CONTENTS

FOREWORD

I LOVED MY WORK as a priest. Whether in parishes or in schools or in community involvement, I enjoyed working not only with my own people but with people and clergy of other religions. I thoroughly enjoyed the spirit of camaraderie generated among us. We worked well together. Some clergy, sadly, kept themselves aloof and chose not to associate with people of other religions, feeling their religion was the true religion and that it would be sinful to give the appearance of endorsing another religion. I suppose that was where we as Catholics were at not very long ago, and where some of us still are. But for those of us who did break out of that crusty shell, we learned to appreciate one another and see how each of us was loved by God and expressed a facet of Jesus the others had overlooked. We were all concerned about our work, about our people, about the exciting and discouraging happenings in our communities.

It took a long time, however, for me to realize that there was something missing in our approach to religion, and this made me feel uneasy. We were sensitive to the customs and traditions of each of our churches. We were aware and concerned about community problems. We, as clergy, were conscientious about protecting our people's faith and their allegiance to their church and synagogue, which we should be. But there was something that did not ring true. One day it struck me that while we were all church- or synagogue-oriented, we did not seem to be sensitive to what might be God's concerns. After all, God is our religion. Churches and synagogues are merely the vehicles of God's message. Their teaching of widely divergent messages impressed me as fragmenting the unity of God's mind, and not reflecting an intelligent, caring God to a world reaching out for comfort and healing. I began to realize it didn't make sense that we were wandering in so many different directions when God's mind is one. Catholics were in love with Church and obsessed with Church laws and customs, and insensitive to those who could not maintain the Church's ideals. Protestants were obsessed with the Bible and their conflicting interpretations of Scripture as well as their own customs and taboos, and were equally insensitive to sinners. Jews were obsessed with keeping their people loyal to their bloodlines, and careful not to let them become too close to Christians. Belief in God often seemed secondary, and sensitivity to God's concerns to be almost nowhere in focus. A synagogue member could be an agnostic or an atheist. That was acceptable, but to become a Christian was unthinkable and meant excommunication, and not very long ago, hanging a crepe on the front door of the person's home was not a rarity. It struck me that God could not be happy with that kind of mentality. These obsessions kept us all, while being ceremoniously friendly, at a safe distance from one another, carefully preserving the invisible walls that divided us, and paying only token homage to any real gesture toward unity. I could not help but feel that what God wished was of little concern. Occasionally, something genuine and beautiful would happen, like what occurred between the local Lutheran parish and our own. The pastor and I became good friends. We did services together. We prayed together. We gathered our congregations together for joint liturgies. We even talked our two bishops into agreeing to co-confirm the children in both our parishes. We were fast approaching real unity. And something similar happened with a local synagogue, Orthodox, no less. We were discussing allowing members of our communities to be members of each other's congregations. Another situation occurred between a local Methodist parish and our own, where we used to speak at each other's service on a regular basis and I would cover for the pastor when he was away.

These situations, however, were the exception. For the most part, we never really took formal steps toward unity. This bothered me deeply because I always felt a need for us all to draw closer to one another. That's what God would want, I thought. We did talk about unity and ecumenism, but rarely were we bold enough to take that giant step toward becoming really one. Unity is a frightening experience when clergy's personal lifestyle and support system is tied to the institution. The hierarchy feel that before unity can become a reality, theologians must agree on a formula, then people would be allowed to become one. It doesn't make sense, because it assumes that just because theologians agree on a formula, the people, like unthinking sheep, will automatically alter their beliefs of a lifetime and accept theologians' formulas. If unity is ever to become a reality, people will have to gather together by charity first, then, as love breaks down the cobweb walls, they will gradually grow to understand Jesus better, and in understanding Him, adopt His vision and understanding, which should be the theological basis for unity.

This realization deepened when it dawned on me one day that although we were involved in our churches, Jesus' interests were, to a great extent, not an element in our decision-making. For Christian leaders, His interests should be foremost, but Church and theology and the demands of canon law had become the primary focus of so many and had practically replaced a sense of Jesus in making decisions. The Bible, on the other hand, had become the religion of the Protestants, as they rejected the teaching authority that originally gave the New Testament Scriptures authenticity. For many Jewish leaders cultural and racial identity had become their religion. God's interests seemed not to be of prime importance, indeed, sometimes they seemed to stand in the way. How else could one explain the horrible religious wars in the former Yugoslavia and Northern Ireland, and South Africa, or the savage meanness in the Holy Land. When I began touring the country, talking about Jesus' life and teaching, I was shocked at the response of people who kept telling me they never heard talks about Jesus' life before. One very holy priest, whom I had known and admired all my life, expressed surprise that I could talk about Jesus for an hour and a half. When I asked him why he was so shocked, he reminded me that we had never been taught about Jesus in the seminary. We were taught theology and scripture and canon law and so many other courses, but no one ever taught any courses about Jesus Himself as a person, and the way He thought and His vision of life.

I got the same response from Protestants. One seminarian for the priesthood told me she had applied to five prestigious seminaries in her denomination before making her decision. She asked the admissions officers at each one if their seminary taught courses about Jesus. She was shocked when the answer each time was "No, but we teach courses on Christology as electives. They are, however, not required." Another Protestant seminarian asked if I would come to his seminary and talk about Jesus. I told him I would be glad to if he arranged with his faculty for an invitation. He told me he would try. I suggested in the meantime that he ask one of the theology professors on staff if he would talk to the seminarians about Jesus. He said he and other students had asked their favorite theology professor. His reply was that he was hired to teach theology, not talk about Jesus.

A few years ago, Dr. John Killinger, a deeply spiritual Southern Baptist theologian, invited me to speak at the Baptist university where he was teaching. It was a beautiful occasion. After the talk, a number of theology professors and ministers thanked me for speaking to them about Jesus. They said they experienced such healing while I was describing a Jesus who was so new to them. They told me that analyzing texts does not necessarily foster a deeper understanding of Jesus. Too late did they realize that knowing scripture was not the same as knowing Jesus. I was touched by their humility.

That explained why there has been such overwhelming response to the Joshua books and the follow-up talks about Jesus. People have a hunger for Jesus and for a genuine understanding of what His Good News really is, whether they are Christians, Jews, Hindus, Buddhists, or even those who cannot identify with any faith. Jesus' Good News responds to the deepest needs of the human soul, no matter what the person's beliefs or lack of belief, and is intimately tied up with our understanding of who Jesus really is and how He thinks and feels. We can never have a proper understanding of His Good News until we know Him as a person, and have watched the subtle psychological effects He had on people to whom He spoke in the villages and on the hillsides of Palestine. When you see Jesus walking so casually among His very human companions, especially people known to be sinners, and notice how comfortable they are in His presence, you realize for the first time that Jesus did not project an image of self-righteousness or as having a critical spirit. So, sinners had the comforting feeling He accepted them as they were and was patient with them as they slowly refocused their sights on more lofty ideals and began to better their lives. That little piece of information alone is a precious part of the Good News because it shows vividly the attitude Jesus reflected toward people who were looked upon as sinners and outcasts. He did not just tolerate them. He accepted their humanness and allowed them to feel relaxed in His presence. Though they had no sense of His divinity, His attitude toward them was different from that of the officials of the religion, who treated them as sinners and breakers of the law. Jesus did not evaluate them in terms of the law. He accepted them as His Father created them—imperfect, defective, limited in understanding, and frightened. He knew their feelings from his own experience, and could appreciate their fears and feelings as fragile human beings. His warmth and friendliness touched them deeply and inspired them to follow His ways. His humble attitude meant a lot to these simple people. They were so used to being looked down upon by those who deemed themselves righteous and religiously correct. They could see Jesus was a holy man and the fact that He liked them drew warm response. He was *genuinely* holy and not at all like the scribes and Pharisees who kept the law but who people sensed were not really godlike, as Jesus was. The people knew Jesus really loved God, and they felt proud that He liked them, too.

We have the same phenomenon in religion today, in all the religions. People so often see religion as people in Jesus' day saw religion, as weighed down with legalities and punishments for violations of religious laws. Religious leaders so often project the image that they are the enforcers of the law, which makes people shy away from them and from religion itself. People crave an encounter with the Good Shepherd, whose interest in them transcended their imperfect observance of religious laws and reached out to them in their weakness and sinfulness. "I am the Good Shepherd. I go out in search for the lost, the bruised, the troubled, and the hurting sheep. When I find them, I pick them up, place them on my shoulders, and carry them back home, because I love the sheep." People need to meet this gentle God today, but so often search in vain for a human reflection of Him. Religious leaders, like the leaders in Jesus' day, are often more concerned about the business of religion, and enforcing laws, and theological correctness than being themselves witnesses to the gentle Shepherd who always taught the highest of ideals, but showed remarkable compassion when people fell far short of those ideals. It is His children who are God's concern, not religion. Only too often it is religion that is clergy's concern, and not the pain and hurt their legalism inflicts on people, which caused Jesus such anguish. When you see some of the unhealthy personalities coming out of the seminaries today, so obsessed with self-importance and rigid legalism, and ecclesiastical correctness, and meticulous attention to dress and personal image, you get the sick feeling that the scribes and Pharisees have come back from the dead. I feel sorry for the healthy ones who will spend so much of their own ministry healing the wounds caused by the others.

Yet, at the same time, we live in an exciting moment of history. We are in the process of reevaluating all our previously accepted values, the very pillars of our civilization. Religion itself, as one of those pillars, is under intense scrutiny, and if we are to evaluate Christianity wisely, we must not just analyze its teachings and moral code, but go to the heart of Christianity, Jesus Himself, and make a humble and prayerful effort to understand Him as a Person, because He *is* our religion, and understand how He thinks because that *is* our theology, and how He lived because that *is* our morality as Christians. Christianity, scripture included, is merely the medium of His message, the vehicle of His Presence in history, as we attempt to know Him.

The following pages represent my own simple portrait of Jesus. Admittedly it is woefully incomplete, but it is an attempt to whet people's appetite to search the mind and heart of Jesus so they can draw close to Him and, in that intimacy, grow to know Him in a way they never thought possible.

Then, from the warmth and intensity of that relationship, deepened by a faithful prayer life, they can channel their own inspired knowledge and understanding of Him to a world that is desperately hungry for Him and the Good News He came to share with us.

A
PORTRAIT
of JESUS

CHAPTER 1

A PORTRAIT OF JESUS

AFTER LIVING IN NAZARETH for thirty years, Jesus began to deliver his message which He called the Good News. It was a sharp title, calculated to jar people into thinking differently about their relationship with God. What was this Good News? In the time of Jesus, people were burdened with layer upon layer of laws that regulated the smallest detail of daily life. Besides the oppressive laws of their Roman conquerors, there was the body of Jewish law, civil and religious. And among the religious laws there were not just ten commandments. There were 613 commandments and 365 prohibitions, and many hundreds lesser injunctions that people had to follow. When they could not measure up to these ideals, the religious leaders excommunicated them and cut them off from the society of "decent" people. St. Paul described the law as the "unbearable burden that no human being could carry."

When Jesus spoke, He was addressing people who were the victims of these burdensome laws. When He spoke in the synagogue at Nazareth, He first read from the scroll that was handed to Him. "The Spirit of the Lord is upon me; because he has anointed me; to bring good news to the poor he has sent me, to proclaim to the captives release, and sight to the blind; to set at liberty the oppressed, to proclaim the acceptable year of the Lord and the day of recompense" (Jn. 4, 18–19). It was not about Roman domination. It was about religious domination.

To the people who heard Him that day, it could not but arouse feelings of hope and expectancy. That was the prophecy from Isaiah, a prophecy that promised a whole new way of life when the Savior came, a way based on freedom from injustice and oppression, religious oppression included, and a thousand years of prosperity.

What was Jesus promising that day? He told people He had come to fulfill that prophecy, to bring them the Good News for which they had waited for so long.

But what was this Good News that Jesus had in mind? What was He promising the people? What was this Good News supposed to mean to them, and to us centuries later? We sing about it in our churches, we talk about it. We repeat the words over and over in sermons, but ask anyone what it means and most Christians would be hard pressed to come up with an adequate answer. What preacher ever attempts to define it? And yet it is the whole reason for Jesus' coming.

During my whole life I have no recollection of anyone ever defining the meaning of Jesus' Good News other than to say Jesus came to save us from our sins and open the gates of heaven for us. Admittedly that is excellent news, but to have meaning for people we cannot just make the statement and leave it at that. What does "save us from our sins mean"? What does "heaven" mean? What are the alternatives? A thousand questions come to mind that need to be answered if we are to appreciate what the Good News really is and what it should mean to us in terms of everyday living.

To understand the Good News and what it is, we have to not just listen to what Jesus says, but watch the way He lives. Most of His messages are hidden in His lifestyle, and particularly in the way He treated people. "I am the light of the world. Come, follow me." "Why are you all so worried and troubled. Stop worrying, your heavenly Father will take care of you." Now, that is tremendous Good News for those who have the childlike trust and openness to accept it. But that is only a small part of the Good News. What else was Jesus offering to the people?

Jesus began proclaiming this Good News not far from Jerusalem, near the Jordan River, where John preached repentance and baptized his followers. Jesus met His first disciples there, Andrew and John. It was at this time that He began to teach and heal. When word got back to Nazareth that He was doing these things, the townsfolk were shocked. "Where did He get all this from? Isn't this the carpenter's son, the boy we grew up with?"

That is a remarkable statement when you think about it. The people who grew up with Jesus and knew Him for thirty years had never seen anything particularly holy in Him during all that time, so they were shocked. And then you ask yourself, "How could Jesus live in that little village for all those years and never give the slightest hint as to His identity?" And the next question pops into your mind: "How could the Son of

God, the living reflection of the God of the Covenant, live in that village for all that time, and not impress people with His holiness, to say nothing of His divinity?''

And the answer can be only that Jesus' idea of holiness was different from their idea of holiness, and *our* idea of holiness. The ideal of holiness in those days was scrupulous observance of the law—loyalty to all the traditions and customs that had become the epitome of accepted Jewish religious life. Apparently Jesus was not known for that, so when He began to talk about spiritual things and to heal, those who knew Him and had grown up with Him were shocked.

It seems obvious that people familiar with Jesus looked upon Him as just an ordinary person. He didn't "put on the pious,'' as my Irish friends used to say. And it is rather interesting that nowhere in the Gospels do any of the Evangelists describe Jesus as religious. One makes the remark that He went about doing good, but he does not refer to Jesus as religious. One can only conclude that Jesus had His own idea of what it meant to be holy or religious, and it did not conform to the accepted norm of those times. It seems that for Jesus, being fully human in the best sense of the word was true holiness; being what God created us to be: just ourselves, good human beings. That's the only explanation as to why they were shocked when Jesus started to preach and to heal. To their way of thinking, He was too earthy and too human to be doing those kinds of things. There is a profound revelation in that, and an important part of the Good News, that you could be just ordinary, doing just the ordinary, everyday things that people do, and underneath that simple, ordinary demeanor possess extraordinary holiness. That is so different from ourselves. When we reach a point in our life and start to take religion seriously, we become so obnoxious, people can't stand us. We feel we have to act holy, and pressure everyone around us to become what we, after many years, have finally become. Jesus apparently was not that way. He did not go around Nazareth asking everyone if they were saved, and forcing religion on people. Jesus was not into religion. He was concerned about relationships, with his Father and with the people. Yet He certainly was concerned about everybody's salvation, but hounding everyone was not His style.

What, then, did people see in Jesus? This is important because how Jesus lived His own life as a human shows how we are to live ours. He is "the way, the truth, and the life" that we are to follow. Apparently Jesus lived simply, just like everyone else in the village. He was deeply in love with everything alive, from God down to the simplest creature, as is so clear in the Gospels. He was "simple as a dove and sly as a fox," as He counseled His apostles to be on one occasion. He was highly intelligent, prudent, circumspect, farseeing, gentle and compassionate, courageous, and not afraid to defend Himself when attacked, as He did so often in His confrontations with the scribes and Pharisees. He was charming and gracious, not prone to anger, never giving an appearance of self-righteousness, but possessing a genuine humility and meekness and an understanding of others. And since we see humor in so much of God's creation, Jesus had to have a wonderful sense of humor, though it shows only when you read between the lines of the Gospels. In short, what people saw in Jesus was a beautifully balanced human being, grown to full potential as a person, and one who was fun to be with.

Obviously, to Jesus, that was His definition of a holy person, an individual who allowed all their God-given uniqueness to grow within to full maturity and in the process becoming a beautiful human being. As simple and ordinary and down-to-earth as He was, He was the holiest Person whoever lived. But people could not recognize it. He was not noted for His attachment to religion and its practices and customs and the "traditions of the ancients" as He described them. Jesus' attachment was to His Father, not to religion, and He was so secure in that love that He did not have to make it obvious. His intimacy with His Father was so finely woven into the fabric of His personality that it did not stand out as a caricature. Nor were the trappings of religion a part of Him. Nor did He wear special clothes like the scribes and Pharisees. What He wore had nothing to do with His relationship with God. He came to simplify the practice of religion, and His view of life was supremely healthy.

From that little statement "Where did he get all this? Is not this the carpenter's son?" we can logically draw a neat picture of the naturalness and casualness of Jesus.

The marriage feast of Cana, however, reveals even more about Jesus, as well as about His mother. In those days, when a girl was born, the father would start making an extra batch of wine each year to prepare for the daughter's wedding some sixteen years down the line; the regular batch for himself, his family, and his friends, and the second batch to prepare for the daughter's wedding. At the wedding reception in Cana, the situation was most probably ordinary. Jesus and Mary were both invited. Mary arrived on time, and even though Jesus came, He was three days late. He obviously felt He should be there, which leads one to believe they were probably relatives. When He arrives, accompanied by His newfound friends the disciples, His mother approaches Him: "Son, they have no wine!" "So what, Mother? What do you expect me to do? My time has not yet come, the time appointed by my Father."

Analyze that scene! The little crowd of merrymakers had finished off a sixteen-year supply of wine in three days. It is easy to assume some were probably not in the best of shape, which Mary could obviously see. Yet, it does not bother her. She is more concerned about the bride and groom being embarrassed for running out of wine when there were still five days left of the wedding party. So Mary quietly approaches Jesus and lets Him know the situation, casually dropping Him a hint. Then you ask yourself, "Now, why would she be dropping Him a hint unless she knew that He could do something? And how would she know that He could do something unless she had seen Him doing tricks around the house."

Mary didn't take His reply as negative. Apparently the whole conversation was not recorded. She goes over to the waiters and tells them, "Do whatever He tells you. (He's got something up His sleeve.)"

"What do you want us to do?" they ask.

"You see those big stone water jars over there?"

"Yes, what about them?"

"Fill them up to the brim!" (to the brim!!!)

Which they proceed to do.

"Now take some to the headwaiter."

When the headwaiter tasted the water made wine, he reprimanded the waiters for saving the best wine until last. "Usually people serve the best wine first, then, when people have been drinking freely, they serve a poorer wine when the guests can't tell the difference." Now, that had to be real wine and not grape juice, because grape juice would not have had that effect on people.

Sit back and think about this for a minute. Jesus can certainly see that some of the guests were not in the best of shape. It apparently did not bother Him. He spots the six stone water jars always kept on hand for ritual purifications, and capable of holding between twenty-five and thirty gallons each. "Fill them up . . . to the brim!" Jesus tells the waiters. Between 150 and 180 gallons of wine, the best of wine, and that was after they had already finished off a sixteen-year supply.

I would have thought twice. I know some clergy who would not have even considered it. It would have been scandalous, approving of such a thing. And here you have the Son of God come down to earth, and it doesn't even bother Him. The only thing that concerned Him was that it was not the time His Father had planned for Him, but then His mother asked Him, so He obliged, and very generously. (A good Scripture quote, by the way, for Mary's intercession with her Son.)

A person certainly cannot use that story as a scriptural argument for drinking too much. Jesus was not rewarding the heavy drinkers. He was showing kindness to the newlyweds. But it does show how down-to-earth and casual Jesus and Mary were, and how comfortable Jesus felt with His very human companions. Since the hosts may have been relatives and most of the people friends whom Jesus had grown up with, it is not far-fetched to imagine some of the more vivacious of His relatives grabbing Jesus by the hand and coaxing Him out onto the dance floor to dance with them the Israelite equivalent of a jig or a polka. I know it may seem shocking to think of this, but perhaps it is because we are not used to thinking of Jesus having fun. Yet, in reading the Gospels carefully, we can see

He did enjoy parties, and was it just to sit in the corner or to talk about serious issues? Not likely.

Seeing Jesus so comfortable among His very human companions reveals much about Him. First of all, He felt comfortable with His humanity. We humans don't enjoy being human. We are ashamed of being human. We are embarrassed by the necessities of our humanity. We are ashamed of our sensitivities. God forbid anyone ever see us cry, at least us men! I have friends I have never seen laugh, maybe giggle in an unguarded moment, but never a hearty belly laugh. It would show a lack of control. Having done so much counseling during my many years of parish work, I was appalled at the number of women who were ashamed to let their husbands know they enjoyed sex, and the number of husbands who have never told their wives they loved them. How sad! We are ashamed of being human, and of opening ourselves to be vulnerable.

I was once at a picnic with some close friends, and one of the fellows was acting like a little kid.

"What got into you, Harry?" I asked him.

"My father just told me he loved me."

"What's so great about that?"

"He never told me before, Father. And he's not even drunk."

"How old are you, Harry?"

"Seventy-five."

"And how old is your father?"

"Ninety-six."

That poor man waited for seventy-five years to hear his father say "I love you," and when he heard it, he jumped around like a little child. As wonderful as it was, it was so sad.

Some children go to their graves without ever having heard

those words from their father's lips, and, sometimes, even from their mother's lips. We are ashamed of being human, of showing tender feelings, of allowing ourselves to be vulnerable. And to see the Son of God at a wedding party having a good time and being so beautifully human and so gracious shows a remarkable facet of the Good News in living color!

CHAPTER 2

A HAPPY MESSIAH?

IT IS REVEALING THAT Jesus chose a wedding party for the launching of His public ministry. And you can be sure word of what He did there spread like wildfire, telling everyone in the surrounding area of His kindness and His remarkable gift to the bride and groom. That seems to have been the message He wanted to precede Him, to disarm people so they would not be afraid of Him. Everything about Jesus spoke of simplicity, being born in a stable, living an unknown existence, showing nothing out of the ordinary except when some need called forth His extraordinary power to heal or to comfort. "Come to me all you are weary and heavily burdened and I will refresh you, for I am meek and humble of heart." How disarming! But that is how Jesus wanted to be known. "Do not be afraid of me," He seems to be saying. "I have come to bring you Good News, to make you happy."

23

It did not take long before this simple preacher aroused the curiosity and almost immediate hostility of the religious leaders. It is strange, because He was devoid of all the trappings of the trouble-making pseudo-messiahs who were springing up like mushrooms. It is hard to understand why the scribes and Pharisees were so disturbed by Him. After all, they were the teaching authority of the Jewish religion, the magisterium, as we would say. (Even Jesus was to recognize that authority later.) One would think they would have been on the lookout for an unusually good person like Him to come upon the scene, because the Messiah's coming was expected at any moment, and they were supposed to be the ones to recognize Him and introduce Him to the people. Furthermore, Jesus' remarkable ability to heal and do good should have alerted them. But the fact that on occasion He healed on the sabbath stopped them short. The sabbath law forbade working on that day. Jesus ignored it. Open-minded religious leaders would have realized that that aspect of the sabbath law did not come from God but was added by their ancestors. Extenuating circumstances could certainly justify exceptions, especially where the crippled and the possessed were concerned. But for some reason, the leaders seemed to have had a bad attitude toward Jesus from the very beginning, and were not disposed to allow for any exceptions. Was it because He never graduated from any of their schools or belonged to one of the more famous families in their elite society. Perhaps, like the prophets, it was because He was teaching on His own and without their endorsement. How could Yahweh pick Him to teach the people when we are the magisterium? Yet that was the way God worked so often throughout Israelite history. He set up the teaching authority, then, when they were not responsive to his messages, He would send prophets outside that magisterium to teach the people. This always infuriated the priests and the scribes, who were so conscious of their God-given authority. Jesus accused these same people in His own day of building the tombs for the prophets whom their ancestors murdered. The religious leaders' attitude toward Jesus was the same. We cannot allow this man to teach like this. We are the teachers. If we allow Him to continue, it will undermine our authority. With that kind of attitude, no matter in what form the Messiah would have come they would have had a problem, because He would have been a threat to their jealously guarded domination over the people. Jesus could not have but felt distressed over this. His Father had carefully guided these teachers through the centuries to shepherd His people just for this occasion. And now that His Son was there, they turned out to be His enemies. He would have to introduce Himself to the people. He would have to do all the work Himself without their help.

That would have been all right, except that they did not leave Him alone. They had spies that dogged His every step, trying to discredit Him among the people, even spreading the rumor that the good works He obviously performed could not come from God. "He just appears to be good, but He is a stumbling block along your paths to trip up and destroy the innocent and unwary. If He appears to be doing remarkable things, remember, Satan can do good things too, and it is clear to us that this Man's power is from Satan."

What a hideous and mean-spirited judgment against a Person who preached only the highest of ideals and spent His days comforting and healing, and His nights in prayer! It is frightening to see such mean-spiritedness among God's chosen. It seems even God's carefully laid plans can be temporarily frustrated by human pettiness.

As difficult and discouraging as this must have been for Jesus, He did not allow Himself to become obsessed with their harassment. He had too much to do, and the accomplishment of His Father's will had to be His prime occupation. His extraordinary discipline kept Him from being distracted by the scribes' and Pharisees' continuous criticisms and harassment as He went about His daily work.

When confronted publicly, however, Jesus never backed off. You get a glimpse of the spunk He must have shown as a boy when bullies in the neighborhood might have started trouble with Him. In confrontations with the scribes and Pharisees, He did not walk away. He fired right back at them. ''Woe to you, scribes and Pharisees, white-washed sepulchers, so nice to look at on the outside, but on the inside full of filth and dead men's bones! You wash the outside of the cup and leave the inside dirty. Woe to you, scribes and Pharisees, hypocrites, you build up heavy burdens and lay them on people's shoulders and don't lift a finger to lighten those burdens, you hypocrites!''

And yet, in spite of the bad scenes between them, the scribes and Pharisees seemed to have sensed that Jesus was concerned about them, and cared for them, so they felt very comfortable inviting Him to their homes for dinner. And He invariably went, like the time Simon, the chief Pharisee in town, invited Him. The man was so proud Jesus accepted his invitation, he invited all the other Pharisees to dine with them. As they were seated, a woman came barging into the dining room, fell down at Jesus' feet, and started to cry, washing His feet with her tears, drying them with her hair, and anointing them with perfumed oil. How intimate! It didn't bother Jesus at all. How beautiful! But Simon's wheels were turning a mile a minute. "Hmmm, how does He know her? If He were what His reputation says He is, He certainly must know what kind of a woman she is."

Knowing just what Simon was thinking, Jesus, with supreme delicacy, said to him, "Simon, I have a little something to say to you."

"Say it, rabbi!"

"When guests are invited to a party, it is the custom for the host to greet the guests at the front door with a kiss, and you did that for all the other guests, but you did not do it for me. That's all right. It is also the custom for the host to provide a bowl of water at the front door so the guests can wash the dust off their feet, and you did that for all the other guests, but you did not do it for me. That's all right too. It is also the custom, since we don't bathe that much, for the host to provide a jar of deodorant at the front door, so the guests can smell presentable at the dinner table. You did that for all the other guests, but you did not do it for me. That's all right too. I took a bath in the Jordan River this morning anyway.

"But look at this woman, Simon. Since she came in, she hasn't ceased to wash my feet with her tears, dry them with her hair, and anoint them with perfumed oil. So I pose this little problem to you, Simon. There was once a very wealthy man (obviously God the Father) who loaned out huge sums of money to two men. To one he loaned a million dollars, to the other he loaned a mere five hundred. Neither could pay him back, so he generously forgave both of them. Which one do you think would love him the more?"

"The one he forgave the more," Simon responded.

"I tell you, Simon, this woman, as many as her sins are, they are forgiven because she loves much." Reading the text in its fullness, it is clear Jesus is also implying that though Simon's sins are few, God has a difficult time with him because he has never learned how to love. And that precisely is the problem Jesus had with the scribes and Pharisees, that though they were totally involved with religion and made a show of their model observance of law, they never learned to love God or to treat people with compassion. "It is compassion I want, not sacrifice."

There is a theology in that little episode that has never been fully developed. Here is a woman, a well-known sinner with this huge debt to God, which we would call mortal sin. And Jesus has the nerve to say, "Her sins, as many as they may be, are forgiven because she loves much."

That is contrary to what all our denominations teach. We all teach that if you commit a serious sin, that sin destroys all the good you ever did and cuts you off from God, destroying your friendship with Him. So often preachers will say, "If you really love God, you won't sin. You cannot be holy and a sinner at the same time." That theology has done untold psychological and emotional, as well as spiritual, damage to so many people.

I will never forget a young man who came to me regularly for confession. He spent much of his free time during the week working with young people, trying to keep them out of trouble and introduce them to Jesus. This young man had a remarkable friendship with Jesus. After confessing his sins, he would break down and cry. I asked him one day why he was crying, and his answer was "Father, I love Jesus so much. Why do I keep falling into the same sins? I spend most of my life cut off from God."

I frankly was at a loss as to what to say to him because that was the theology we were all taught. This fellow knew his theology well. If I knew then what I learned only recently from Jesus' words in Simon the Pharisee's house, I could have said to him, "Son, don't worry, you are not cut off from God. Your sins, as many as they may be, are forgiven because God sees how much you love Him and how you reach out to your troubled and hurting neighbors. So you are still God's friend." That would have made good theological sense because it was Jesus' own words under similar circumstances.

Then I thought of Peter. I don't think any of us will ever love Jesus the way Peter loved Jesus, yet until the day we die, we hope we will never commit the kind of sin that Peter committed, denying that he ever knew Jesus, and only a few minutes after he had made his first Communion at the Last Supper.

And I asked myself, "Was Peter still Jesus' friend?" Of course he was. You don't think Jesus' love is that superficial or fickle? Friendship doesn't end just because we do stupid things, especially out of weakness. Jesus merely knew better than ever that He had a coward for a friend. But that's all right; all Jesus' friends limp or are seriously defective in some way. It doesn't seem to bother Him. That is what is so extraordinary about God's love. Our making God like ourselves is what has done so much damage to people. And theologians have done no better job than the rest of us in communicating this image of God to people.

In fact, the theology that Jesus is trying to get across by that episode in Simon's house is that "my Father did not intend to create you as little gods. He created each of you to do just a little job, and gave you the gifts and talents we need to do that little job. The rest of your personality may be imperfect and incomplete, which means that you are going to make mistakes and fall short of your ideal of being good, and, in short, fall into sin." Jesus reminds the Pharisees of how God views people. "This woman, as many as her sins are, they are forgiven because she loves much." He also seemed to be saying, "Simon, as few as your sins are, God has a hard time because you have never learned how to love." Jesus could see that woman's quiet, desperate reaching out to God, and her secret caring for troubled and needy neighbors. Her real, genuine love of God and care for others far outweighed her well-known breaches of God's law. And He assured them all, and the woman too, that she was still God's friend. This must have been like an electric shock to those smug Pharisees, who considered themselves the epitome of holiness, the ideals of righteousness. That story fits in so perfectly with the story of the Pharisee and the publican, which was the subject of another encounter of Jesus with the religious elite.

One day the question was brought up by some Pharisees as to who was pleasing to God.

Jesus responded by saying, "Two men went to the temple to pray. One was a Pharisee, the other a publican. The Pharisee walked straight up through the sanctuary, right up before the tabernacle, and with arms outstretched, said, 'I thank you, God, that I am not like the rest of men, adulterers, extortioners, thieves, or like that publican back there. I fast twice a week, I pay tithes on all I possess.' "

Then Jesus continued. "The publican, standing down in the

back of the temple, could hardly raise his eyes to heaven but merely beat his breast and said, 'God, be merciful to me. I am a sinner.' "

Jesus then added, "That publican went back home justified, while the Pharisee went out of the temple rejected by God."

Now, that truly is a shocking statement, that a man who kept the law so perfectly could be rejected by God, when we were all brought up to believe that if you kept the law, you would be pleasing to God. If keeping the commandments does not make us pleasing to God, what, then, does? And Jesus answers that question when He is confronted by an expert in the law on another occasion.

One day, a lawyer came up to Jesus to test Him. "Rabbi, what is the greatest commandment of the law?" A simple enough question, until you realize there were not only ten commandments, but 613 commandments, and one of the most hotly debated issues was which was the greatest.

Jesus' answer was stunning. "The first commandment is 'Love the Lord your God with your whole heart, with your whole soul, with your whole mind, and with all your strength.' The second is like it. 'Love your neighbor as you love yourself.' On these two is based the whole law and the prophets."

"You have answered rightly, rabbi, but my question is 'Who is my neighbor?' "

Jesus then proceeds to tell a little story. "A man was going down from Jerusalem to Jericho, and he fell among thieves. They beat him, robbed him, and left him lying there, half dead.

"A priest went down the road and saw the man lying there

and walked right by. Then, a Levite (a temple attendant) went down the road and saw the man lying there, and he, too, walked right by.

"Then a stranger happened to be going down the road, saw the man lying there, and felt compassion for him. He got off his horse, took out a flask of oil and wine and cleaned out the man's wounds, put his own cloak on him, put him on his horse, and took him down to an inn. Paying the innkeeper, he instructed him to take care of the man, and promised to pay whatever he owed him over and above, on his return journey."

Jesus then added, "And he was a Samaritan. Now, tell me, who showed himself a neighbor to the man?"

The lawyer responded sheepishly, since the Jews hated the outcast Samaritans, "The one who showed mercy."

"Go and do likewise!"

In this parable Jesus answered that most difficult question: Who is pleasing to God? It is not necessarily the one who is dedicated to religion with its traditions and practices or accurate understanding of religious teachings, but the person who cultivates love and compassion toward others, including God. With the sharpness of a laser beam, He cuts through all the crust and nonsense concocted through the centuries and touches the very core of what religion really is: our relationship with God. Even though you may be weak, are you focused on God, are you sensitive to the pain and hurt all around you? This is the essence of the person who is pleasing to God. Not that accuracy in belief and disciplining human weakness are not important, but loving the Father in heaven and caring for others is absolutely essential. They were the teachings that were critical to Jesus. Jesus realized few people will ever have an accurate understanding of the nature of God and even the identity of the Son of God, but He knew that it was within the heart of everyone to care for others. One might even wonder if the apostles themselves understood the Eucharist Jesus was giving them at the Last Supper. It seems they did not even have a clear understanding of his divinity until long after the Resurrection. One might wonder if Jesus shouldn't have been a bit more theologically correct!

The problem with the scribes and Pharisees was that they canonized doctrine and law and overlooked essential goodness and compassion. When they witnessed this sheer goodness in Jesus, it must have been such an indictment of their hypocrisy and shallow spirituality, they could not but hate Him. They were driven to do whatever they had to rid themselves of Him.

As much as the scribes and Pharisees tried to aggravate Jesus, He never allowed Himself to be thrown off balance or become paranoid over them. Watching Him on His daily travels, you see a Man who is calm and self-possessed and rarely ruffled. He is relaxed and casual. He appears in a village in the morning, just passing through, and people see Him. Word spreads that He is in town and the crowds pour into the streets looking for Him. Soon the blind, the crippled, the possessed, the curious, surround Him, so there is hardly room to breathe. He leads them outside the village to an open space and directs them to spread out on a grassy knoll and relax. He then spends the next hour or so telling them about the Good News of the Kingdom. They sit spellbound. Pharisees or their spies mill around the fringes of the crowd, seething with envy at His genius in touching people's hearts, and holding huge crowds in thrall. His message is so simple, yet He reaches to the very essence of people's relationship with God.

Seeing Jesus with the common people is seeing Jesus at His best. It is interesting that He seemed to feel most at home with just ordinary, simple people. We might call them sinners and feel uncomfortable with them. Jesus knew these people and what they were like. He fashioned them. He knew their good traits as well as the nasty hidden side of their personalities, and yet He still enjoyed associating with them. He seemed to genuinely enjoy their companionship. Walking through the back streets in Old Jerusalem, He saw and smelled all the sights and odors of a crowded, poorly ventilated marketplace filled with people who may not have washed recently. Those back streets are not much different today than they were in Jesus' day, filled with vendors and their seemingly endless line of booths offering anything that would appeal to human fancy. Chunks of raw meat, covered with flies, hang from hooks at one booth. Fish just caught that morning in the Sea of Galilee lie in piles or in baskets next to boxes full of dried and salted fish at another booth. Next to that, at still another booth, are baskets full of vegetables and fruit. Jesus walks through the crowded alley, rubbing elbows with people along the way, stopping to talk to this one or that one, helping a little child crying because she lost her mother and cannot find her in the crowd. He was always very much a part of the people's lives. They saw Him not as some great, high-minded religious reformer ever ready to indict people for their sins and violations of doctrine. They saw Him as one of themselves, simple, earthy, with a ready laugh at something funny that happened, and not prone to find fault with people's weaknesses and idiosyncrasies, and crude, sometimes bawdy humor.

I think that was one trait that stands out in Jesus, His acceptance of people where they were at. He made them. He enjoyed them. When you read the Gospels carefully, you never see Jesus criticizing anyone. It is true He tore the scribes and Pharisees apart, but not for their weaknesses. He was angry with them for what they had done to religion, for having stripped the joy and spontaneity out of people's relationship with God and reduced that relationship to a nightmare of endless religious laws and rituals that no one could possibly endure, as St. Paul complained.

Religious reformers are often high-strung, angry people who make others feel uncomfortable in their presence. They are quick to find fault, to point out people's sins, and to isolate them from "nice" people. They are quick to anger when others do not share their vision. You don't see that in Jesus. With his vastly comprehensive vision of life in all its facets and deep sense of mission, there is no hint of obsession or paranoia. It is a subtle indication of his divinity. His relaxed casualness is disarming. People enjoyed being near Him. When He walks down the street, there is either a group of children with Him, or an entourage of townsfolk, many of them well known for their unsavory reputations. They felt proud in knowing Jesus enjoyed their company. He obviously did not act piously or preach religion to them. They would have walked away. They were attracted to Him because they sensed a joy and peacefulness that was unusual, and also felt He really liked them. They certainly were not drawn to Him because He exuded religion or righteousness. His own goodness was what ultimately inspired them to change their lives, though not necessarily overnight. His patience with them as they gradually grew to understand Him and even more slowly adopt His way of thinking is a remarkable trait in Jesus.

This is particularly evident in His relationship with the

apostles. Their little group always appears to be so laid back, their conversations so far removed from Jesus' way of thinking. One day, as Jesus and the apostles were walking along, the apostles were arguing among themselves as to who was the greatest among them. Jesus must have been walking a little ahead, seemingly half chuckling, half disappointed. If He were closer, they certainly would not have been expressing themselves so freely. Jesus just let them talk, gradually slowing down until they caught up with Him. Then He casually asked them, "What were you talking about back there?" as if He didn't know.

They were too embarrassed to answer. He did not press the issue, but merely remarked, "You know, important people of this world like to make their importance felt and lord it over their subjects. It cannot be that way with you. Whoever wants to be the greatest among you must be willing to serve the rest." How gentle, how uncritical, how careful not to humiliate or shame them. The apostles were simple folk, unlettered, crude, and Jesus knew what He could reasonably expect from them. But He had chosen them to be the leaders of His disciples one day, and it was important that they exercise their authority gently and with humility, just the way He did. As important as this lesson was for them, He taught the lesson so as not to humble or hurt them. It reveals the delicacy with which Jesus treated people, and helps us to see why people felt so comfortable in His presence.

It was the same with the people who came to Him in such vast numbers. They crowded around Him like little children, hungry to hear words of comfort or encouragement that fell like honey from His lips. It is easy to picture Jesus talking to a crowd quietly about the kingdom of heaven or about trusting

His Father while healing a poor, unfortunate cripple or a man blind from birth, then walking down the street, where He stops to talk to another group as they go about their work.

Another intriguing facet of Jesus' manner of relating to people is His naturalness. So often religious people are obsessed with others' need for salvation, and are insistent they make a commitment to Jesus as Savior. You don't see that obsessive impatience to sell religion that so often characterizes people who have finally found religion. This is noticeable in the brief encounter Jesus had one day with the royal official from Capharnaum. The man heard Jesus was in Cana and went to plead with Him to heal his son, who was at the point of death. A preacher might first demand a commitment of faith in Jesus as Lord and Savior. But not Jesus. He did make the remark, "Unless you see signs and wonders you do not believe," but it was a passing commentary more on the curious multitude standing around than an attempt to convert the man.

Nor was the man offended. He merely pleaded, "Sir, come down before my child dies."

"Go home, your son lives," Jesus told him.

On the way home, the man was met by a courier who told him his son was better. It happened at the same time as Jesus told him "your son lives."

The man and his whole household did believe in Jesus after that, but it came spontaneously and not because Jesus insisted on it.

This naturalness in relating to people manifests the respect Jesus has for the freedom God had given to people. He points to people what is available to them, and by the beauty of His own life shows them how beautiful *their* lives could be if they are willing to follow in His steps. To the rich young man who one day asked Jesus what he had to do to be saved, Jesus merely answered, "Keep the Commandments!" When the young man answered that he had done that from his youth, Jesus then said, "Well, if you want to be perfect, sell what you have, give to the poor, and come follow me!" That was only a suggestion because the man seemed disappointed over Jesus' first answer. It is a total surprise seeing Jesus so detached from people's response to what He offers them, but it shows His respect for people's free will. He realizes some are ripe for conversion, some are far from ready, and, perhaps, some will never be ready.

CHAPTER 3

A SIGN OF CONTRADICTION

ONE OF THE MOST striking phenomena in the Gospels is the endless confrontations between Jesus and the religious authorities. I, like all of us, have read those episodes for years, but it made little impression on me until a few years ago as to how large a segment of the Gospels those confrontations occupy. I am aware some modern Christian and Jewish scholars doubt that these confrontations ever took place, but they are so intricately tied in with the many messages Jesus taught during those rapid-fire exchanges that I find it difficult to doubt the veracity of those episodes. Indeed, an integral part of the Good News is expounded during these exchanges, which start out very early in Jesus' ministry.

In a way, Jesus lays out His mission statement on one occasion when He discusses His relationship to the Law. "I have not come to destroy the Law but to fulfill it. Amen, I say to you, till heaven and earth pass away, not one jot or tittle of the Law will be lost until it is all fulfilled. . . . Unless your justice exceeds that of the scribes and Pharisees, you shall not enter the kingdom of heaven.''

Then Jesus goes on to proclaim that goodness is not in the external observance of commandments, but in the spirit that inspires the proper observance of the Law. A person can keep all the commandments, yet never do one good act. Commandments are negative. They tell you what not to do. Jesus was positive. He promulgated a new law, a law based on love. ''If you are offering your gift at the altar, and you remember your brother has anything against you, leave your gift on the altar, and go first and be reconciled with your brother. Then come and offer your gift'' (cf. Mt. 6).

In Jesus' day the law of retribution was in vogue, ''an eye for an eye and a tooth for a tooth.'' If one injured you, you had a right to take revenge. Jesus' holiness countered that. ''But, I say to you, do not resist the evildoer. On the contrary, if someone strikes you on the one cheek, offer him the other. . . . You have heard it said, 'You shall love your friend and hate your enemy.' But, I say to you, love your enemies, do good to those who hate you. Pray for those who persecute and calumniate you, so you may be children of your Father in heaven, who makes His sun rise on the good and the evil, and sends rain on the just and the unjust. . . . You therefore are to be perfect, even as your heavenly Father is perfect.''

In those few words Jesus outlines His understanding of goodness. Perfection as God is perfect is not in observance of laws and commandments. God does not observe laws or commandments. God's perfection is in His love. It is His essence. God *is* love, and whoever is of God is inspired by love. We are to become perfect in loving the Father and in caring for one another. That is why, in the only example Jesus gave of the Last Judgment, He does not use the Commandments as the basis for judgment, but "Come, blessed of my Father, when I was hungry, you gave me food; when I was thirsty, you gave me drink, etc."

It was not only the people of His day, but it is so common for people of all times to just keep commandments and church laws and observe the externals of religion. In living this way, we miss the point of what worship of God really is, falling each day more deeply in love with God, expressing that love by our sensitivity to the pain and hurt around us, and reaching out to help others, even strangers. To a person who has found God, no person, ever again, is a stranger. In that is the perfection of love, the kind of love that God is, a love that knows no strangers.

A strikingly large portion of the Gospel story relates the dramatic unfolding of that mission statement. The conflict between the scribes and Pharisees and the Good Shepherd is the tension between those obsessed with inflexible insistence on the letter of the law regardless of the damage inflicted on people, and the Good Shepherd, who went out in search of the bruised and hurting sheep driven away by the self-righteous. "The scribes and Pharisees have sat on the chair of Moses. All that they command you, therefore, observe and do. But do not imitate them, for they talk but do nothing. They bind together heavy and oppressive burdens and lay them on people's shoulders, but do not lift a finger to lighten those burdens" (cf. Mt. 23).

The Good Shepherd, on the other hand, goes out looking for the lost, the troubled, and the bruised and hurting sheep, and when He finds them, He picks them up, places them on His shoulders, and carries them back home because He loves the sheep.

The dichotomy is dramatic, because Jesus acknowledges the authority of the scribes and Pharisees. They were the magisterium, the teaching authority appointed by God. Jesus told His disciples to obey them. He then calls the scribes and Pharisees "blind guides who strain out the gnat but swallow the camel," and "blind guides leading the blind, and both fall into the pit."

When He refers to Himself as the Good Shepherd, He places Himself in a role that is in direct contrast to the way religious authorities treated people. They drove the sheep away by excommunicating them and treating them harshly when they broke the religious laws. The same thing happens wholesale to this very day. The Good Shepherd, on the other hand, goes out in search of those who have been driven out. When He finds them wandering aimlessly, hurt and bruised, He gently picks them up, binds up their wounds, and carries them back home.

You see that same theme weaving its way through the rest of the Gospels, as it is developed, refined, and clarified until it becomes clear as polished crystal what Jesus is trying to teach and which is the essence of the Good News. "I have come to save, not to alienate and abandon."

The incident of the apostles walking through the field of grain reflects another facet of that same message. It was a sabbath day. The apostles were hungry. They were taking the heads off the grain and eating them like peanuts. The Pharisees seemed to have jumped out of the grain fields, ready to accuse. "Look at your disciples! They are breaking the sabbath."

Jesus' reply jolted them. "Have you never read what David did when he and his men were hungry—how he entered God's house and took and ate the holy bread and gave it to his men, even though only the priests were allowed to eat it? The sabbath was made for man and not man for the sabbath. The Son of Man is Lord even of the sabbath."

That brief encounter opens up a whole new insight into the purpose of religious law. The showbread was sacred. It symbolized the living presence of Yahweh in the midst of the community. It was for the Jews as sacred as the Eucharist is for Christians. In fact, it prefigured the Eucharist. No Jew would dare touch the showbread, as no Catholic would dare break open the tabernacle and take the Eucharist for lunch. It is shocking to hear Jesus justifying David's actions. Yet it expresses Jesus' attitude toward law. Law is only a support to guide and assist God's children. It is not to be an oppressive burden. It must be responsive to human need. "The law was made for man, not man for the law, the sabbath was made for man, not man for the sabbath" (cf. Mk. 3 and Lk. 6). Where there is a human need the law must bend. It is God's children who are sacred to God, not laws. Laws are to protect or assist God's children. If a law does not do that, it should be reevaluated, and, perhaps, abrogated.

One cannot help but think of religious laws and customs today that may have had a meaning at one time but are a hindrance to the healthy practice of spirituality in our times. This is not to say that morality should change, but there are many religious laws that have nothing to do with the moral law. They are merely arbitrary ordinances that could be changed. Often people's attachment to traditions and customs resist changing them even though they may cause or occasion untold damage to many good people. When religious leaders see the damage done, one would think as good shepherds concerned for the sheep they would be the first to recognize the need for change. It is difficult to understand their obsessive attachment to customs and practices when they more often give rise to scandal than inspire goodness. It might do well for religious leaders of all the denominations to reevaluate practices that are totally out of sync with the mind and spirit of Jesus, and which many good people no longer observe because they know they are foreign to the mind of Jesus. That was the basis for the constant conflicts between Jesus and the religious leaders of His day. They enforced laws that long since had lost their meaning. They incessantly concocted new prohibitions and threatened God's punishment if people did not observe them. It is hard to understand why religious leaders do not see they are doing the same thing today Jesus condemned in the scribes and Pharisees. They would rather police people's lives than guide, instruct, counsel, heal, and inspire the way Jesus did. There is more damage done to people's faith by mean-spirited religious leaders than by the marginal ideas of suspect theologians whose writings few people read anyway. I can think of only a few persons whose faith was damaged by theologians, but I know tens of thousands who have left their faith because of the narrowness and meanness of clergy obsessed with enforcing doctrine and laws. They seem to have an aversion to discuss and arrive at an understanding, and would rather decree and punish. The Good Shepherd loved the sheep and went out to bring them home. The hired hands ruled the sheep with meanness and drove them away. Jesus could teach the highest of ideals, but when people fell short of those ideals, He dealt with them compassionately. The others punished when they were not obeyed and cared little about the damage done to the people's lives and people's faith. That is the great sin in all religion.

CHAPTER 4

A HUMBLE, CASUAL SAVIOR?

IF THE RELIGIOUS OFFICIALS of His day were snobbish and stuffy, Jesus was anything but that. Having created human nature, Jesus knew how to be human, and when you read between the lines of the Gospels, you see a Man who is wonderfully human. You never see Him stiff or locked inside Himself, beset with anxieties, though He daily faced difficulties the best of us could never handle. He seems to almost glide along as if He had not a care in the world. As concerned as He was about spreading His Good News, He is not compulsive or driven like so many people with a mission. He lived His life, enjoying each day, making new friends, and maintaining warm relationships with His old friends. This, too, could be considered part of His Good News. He taught by His example how people could live with joy and serenity, and not allow themselves to be so driven that they lose their peace of mind and sense of balance; and through it all they can enjoy an intimate relationship with God which is built into the essence of being fully human.

Jesus' relationship with the apostles shows this in so many ways. The way the group was organized is fascinating. The first two disciples Jesus did not even pick. Of course, He really did pick them, but the way it was done seemed as if they discovered and picked Him. One day John the Baptizer pointed Jesus out to two of his followers as the Lamb of God. They started to follow Jesus. When He noticed them following Him, He turned and asked them what they wanted and why there were following Him. A natural enough question when you are being followed by two strangers. They asked Him where He lived and His response was "Come and see." I don't know where He showed them. He was over a hundred miles from home at the time. But they stayed with Him that day. The two were impressed with Jesus and could not wait to tell their brothers, Simon and James. From that day on, the four never left Him. How wonderfully casual and natural!

The next day they were leaving for Galilee and came across a man named Philip. "Follow me," Jesus said to him. Just like that. You cannot help but wonder if they had ever met before. If they did, it would make sense. If they hadn't, it is hard to understand the influence Jesus had on a total stranger. Whichever way it was, Philip was impressed and could not wait to tell his friend, Nathaniel, that they had found the Messiah. Nathaniel laughed when Philip said He was from Nazareth. "What good can come out of Nazareth?" was his cynical response.

"Just come and see," Philip insisted, which he did.

When they found Him, Jesus remarked, "Behold a real Israelite in whom there is no guile!"

"How do you know me? You never even met me!" was again his curt reaction.

"Before Philip called you, when you were under the fig tree, I saw you." Fig trees have supple, low-hanging branches with big leaves. It is hard to imagine what someone would be doing under a fig tree. Well, Philip was impressed that Jesus knew, and the others probably laughed at his embarrassment. Perhaps, a hint of Jesus' playful spirit, especially with the apostles, who by now were beginning to bond with one another into very close relationships.

This playful side of Jesus' intimacy with the apostles is a facet of His life I never took much notice of until recently. It happened quite by accident.

I had been invited to speak in Kalamazoo by Sr. Dorothy Ederer, a Dominican sister, and Fr. John Grathwohl, campus ministers at Western Michigan University. The parish was a lively place at that time, with almost three thousand young people coming to Mass on a more or less regular basis. It was one of those rare places that welcomed college students and made them feel a closeness to God. Sr. Dorothy had been using the Joshua books as a way of introducing the college students to Jesus. The books touched them deeply, and they began introducing Joshua to their friends and families. These students were not just churchgoers. They were a beautiful community of caring young people who did a lot of wonderful things for one another and for people in need in the community. I have never seen the likes of such a group of young college students, and I have been on many college campuses.

However, when I found out that Sr. Dorothy spent a lot of her time playing golf, and Rollerblading, and going to movies and wedding receptions and other parties, I was shocked. I asked her when she worked. I was only joking, because it was obvious she was doing an excellent job. I guess I hurt her feelings, and tears began to show in her eyes. She said, "I guess I work best when I play. Perhaps, that's why the kids come to me with all their problems."

When I went back home, I was still thinking about the incident and it made me wonder if there was any of that playful spirit in Jesus. I went through the Gospels again and was surprised to observe how many times Jesus went to parties and dinners. This is all the more exciting, since the Gospels tell only the barest essentials of Jesus' life, and they mention these dinners so often. Apparently, the Gospel writers were also surprised enough at His playfulness to mention it so frequently. It would almost seem that if someone wanted to spend some time with Jesus, the thing to do was to gather a group of friends for dinner and invite Jesus. It seems He would always come, whether it was for Him a chance to expound on the Kingdom or just to enjoy companionship. It was probably both.

One day, Jesus was entering the city of Jericho. A diminutive man, the town's chief tax collector by the name of Zacchaeus, had never been able to see Jesus because he was so short. He decided to climb up into a tree overlooking the street so when Jesus passed by he would finally catch sight of Him.

When Jesus approached, he stopped, looked up into the tree, and said, "Zacchaeus, come down. I am going to stay at your house today." What nerve! Inviting Himself to stay at the house of a total stranger and dine with him!

Zacchaeus was thrilled. The people were scandalized. The little man scurried down the tree, so proud and excited that this famous man was coming to visit him that he said all kinds of things, spewing promises he could not possibly fulfill. He could not believe that this holy man would stoop so low as to come to his home for dinner. He knew full well the reputation he had and what the surrounding crowd thought of him. When he saw the people muttering to one another that Jesus was staying with the likes of him, he promised publicly to give half of his belongings to the poor and to pay back fourfold what he had unjustly taken from people.

Did Jesus invite Himself to dinner just so He could talk seriously to the man? I doubt it. If He wanted to talk seriously, all He had to do was take him aside or talk to him right then and there or arrange to talk with him at some other time. Jesus was never averse to talking to someone about serious things with a crowd standing around. If He did not do it in front of everybody, He took the person aside and talked privately. It was often the only chance He got to touch people's hearts.

This inviting Himself to dinner seems to have been nothing more profound than wanting to have a party and a chance to meet some of Zacchaeus' friends, other outcasts like himself, extortioners. Jesus knew His gesture of kindness would touch their hearts, and encourage them to change their ways. These men were hated because they gouged the people of exorbitant amounts of money in arbitrary taxes they imposed, pocketing most of it for themselves, as the Roman authorities demanded only a percentage of their take. If Jesus wanted to meet sinners, this was the place to meet them, big ones, the kind He really was out to save.

Whether it was on this occasion or on the occasion of another dinner party, Jesus was confronted by a group of Pharisees who were complaining about His lifestyle and His socializing with outcasts. "I cannot understand you people," Jesus lashed out at them. "John came neither eating nor drinking and you called him a fanatic, and possessed by the devil. I come acting normal and you call me a wine bibber, a glutton, a partygoer, and one who hangs around with sinners."

What a stunning observation! Here is the Son of God come down to earth and fully aware that He has a bad reputation. Or, looking at it from an even more shocking point of view, here is the God of the Hebrew Scriptures, Yahweh Himself, come down to earth, the so-called frightful, vindictive God who could slay twenty to thirty thousand people overnight because they crossed Him. Here He is and His own teaching authorities accuse Him of being a drunkard, a glutton, a partygoer, and one who hangs around with sinners.

The interesting thing is that it was not the ordinary common people who gave Jesus this reputation, but the religious leaders, people who were in love with religion and obsessed with doctrinal purity and the rigid observance of law. Religion was their business. Maybe that was their problem, spending their lives making religion work (in their favor). They were the ones who gave Jesus the bad reputation. He indicted them for their obsession with religion but having no love in their hearts for God, and no compassion for people. Traditions and rituals were the gods they worshipped.

It was a surprise seeing this happy, playful side of Jesus' personality. You can be sure that even though it was part of his strategy to gather people to Himself, his socializing was not affected or artificial. It must have been that He really enjoyed the excitement of human comradeship. He obviously was a very sociable person. When you begin thinking of this side of Jesus, it does make sense. Sociability is an expression of love and the enjoyment of friendship. With Jesus' immense love for people, it is only logical that He should have had a wonderful time at family gatherings and friends' parties. This would also explain the naturalness of Jesus in His dealings with people. He showed none of the carefully guarded, "proper" behavior, or stuffiness of so many religious leaders.

This naturalness is part of the warp and woof of Jesus' lifestyle, and the signature of His ministry. Whereas the scribes and Pharisees, and religious leaders after them, instill religious doctrines and customs and rituals into people, and mold them accordingly, Jesus showed no concern for these things. He did share His identity, and His relationships with the Father and the Holy Spirit, but this sharing of His inner life was the expression of His love. He was not teaching or formulating a doctrine to be memorized. His doctrine was in the relationships he was sharing. He was sharing the intimacy of His own relationship with the Father and the Holy Spirit, and introducing His closest disciples to His inner life. We have turned this beautiful sharing of love into finely chiseled and polished doctrines. He did not teach doctrines to be memorized, but shared Himself. He was concerned about sharing His understanding of life with people, and His understanding of God, and of the relationship God's children should have with one another, and that we have been created in such a way that we need each other for the sharing of resources and gifts and talents God has parceled out to each of us in different ways. Deepening of our intimacy with God, caring for one another, was for Jesus true religion. "Caring for widows and orphans" was Jesus' symbolic way of expressing it. It was not that Jesus shunned temple worship or formal religious training that was so essential to a well-informed and balanced understanding of God and how God has worked in people's lives throughout history, but, for Him that was not religion. That was community sharing its past experiences of Yahweh's love and care. It was the vehicle for the community as a family to offer its gratitude and worship to Yahweh, and the vehicle for sharing divine teachings.

That precisely was the nub of the crisis between Jesus and the religious leaders. For them, observing the feasts and the rituals and the perfect observance of the law was religion. For Jesus, it was loving God and caring for people and appreciating the wonderful creation God has blessed us with.

As a result of this continuous wrangling between Jesus and the scribes and Pharisees, we see Jesus spelling out in shocking detail His analysis of the way the law and the ritual was imposed on people in His day. He knew the sabbath rest was His Father's gift to the Jewish people, and a way of protecting slaves from being worked to death. Over time, the religious leaders turned it into a nightmare, stripping all the fun out of this day of worship and family enjoyment. No cooking, no sewing, no helping people in need, no brushing your teeth or washing out your mouth, no playing that demanded physical exertion, no walking more than was absolutely necessary, minute definition of what you could and could not do on this day of family recreation. All this Jesus ignored publicly. To the Pharisees it was nothing more than manifest contempt for the law. Jesus' endless walking from place to place on the sabbath galled them. His curing sick people on the sabbath was an audacious affront to their authority. Not only did it make them look ridiculous in the eyes of the people, but His spunk endeared Him to the people.

When questioned on it by officials, Jesus tore into them for their hypocrisy and their diabolical twisting of His Father's law into a living nightmare. While recognizing their teaching authority instituted by God, He warned the people publicly to beware of them. "The scribes and Pharisees have sat on the chair of Moses. All things that they command you, observe and do. But do not follow their ways. They talk but do nothing. They bind together heavy and oppressive burdens, and lay them on people's shoulders, but do not lift a finger to lighten those burdens."

Even to their faces He did not flinch in exposing their hypocrisy. "Woe to you, scribes and Pharisees, hypocrites! You pay tithes on mint, anise, and cumin but ignore the weightier matters of the law like justice and mercy and faith. These are the things you should observe, while not overlooking the others. Blind guides! You strain out the gnat, but swallow the camel."

This attitude Jesus had toward the law, and how it was imposed, is important for us to understand in depth because it represents a radical departure from the way religion had been taught from the beginning of religion itself. Religion had always been taught as a system of commandments that had to be scrupulously observed if a person wanted to be pleasing to God and to earn whatever reward God had in store for them in some possible future existence. Being pleasing to religious superiors was just as important, as they were custodians of the Law. To disobey them was to disobey God.

Unfortunately, it is still that way. I will never forget a horrible disagreement I had with a bishop many years ago. He had ordered me to do something with which I had serious reservations. I told him I had a problem with it, and that I could not in conscience do it. Angrily, he said to me, "Your conscience is to do what I tell you."

Hurt, I replied, probably in not a nice tone of voice, "I am sorry, bishop, but you are not God."

That is so often the attitude of religious officials, no matter what their denomination or religion. They will form people's consciences, and all the people have to do is obey. You see that mentality not only in the Catholic Church, but in Islam, and in various Christian denominations. Even in those denominations that say they follow the Bible alone. It is not the Bible they follow, but the rigidly enforced interpretations of their minister, or the decrees of their governing bodies. They may not have popes in their religion, but their leaders often wield a control much more demanding than any pope, and over the details of people's daily lives. Woe to any who dare question their authority! How many times have Fundamentalist or Evangelical friends told me, "But our minister told us this is what that text means, or this is what we must do." And they wouldn't dare question it. That is not fidelity to scripture. That is control, and it is totally opposed to the freedom of the children of God that Jesus gave us.

In Jesus' day, the high priests and scribes exercised that kind of authority over the people. The Jewish religion consisted of 613 commandments, 365 prohibitions, and another 365 that refined and protected the observance of the others. As in our own day, when people could not live up to the ideals, they were punished in various ways, and to varying degrees, often by being cut off from the community. Nice people were not allowed to associate with them.

The 365 commandments and all the lesser laws and prohibitions may seem like a lot, but when you consider that civil law and religious law were mingled, it does not seem terribly unreasonable when you compare it with all the laws we have today, civil and religious combined. St. Paul still makes the remark that Jesus came to free us from "the unbearable burden of the law which no human being could carry." St. Paul realized fully the import of Jesus' attitude toward the law. The first council of the Church in Jerusalem was held to resolve serious issues involving observance of the law.

Some three hundred years later we see St. Augustine refusing to allow the catechists in his diocese in North Africa to teach the Ten Commandments. I first learned that in a Knights of Columbus pamphlet about Jesus and the Law. The reason St. Augustine gave to his catechists was that the Ten Commandments as such were not a part of Christianity. The substance of the Commandments was the natural law Christians had to observe, but only because the natural law was the unwritten law in everyone's heart. Besides, most of the Commandments were negative; "Thou shalt not . . ." Jesus gave His followers a new commandment; "Love one another as I have loved you!" which was a refinement of what He said at another time; "Love God with your whole heart and soul, and your neighbor as yourself. On these is based the whole law and the prophets." Jesus' whole approach to religion was positive, ever emphasizing love, love of God, and love of one's neighbor.

A person taught that the Commandments are the ultimate moral guide might object; "If you cannot use the Commandments as the basis for morality, what do you use as a foundation for healthy moral judgment? How could Jesus' simple injunction to love God and one another possibly be sufficient?"

It is noteworthy that St. Augustine eventually did give in, because his catechists complained that they could not teach new converts moral values unless they could use the Ten Commandments as a guide. He compromised and told them they could use them, not in their negative form, but in a positive way, as ten expressions of love. If you really love God, this is how you will treat Him. If you really love your neighbor, this is how you will treat your neighbor.

Even though Jesus abrogated the old law, He did have a firm set of principles for making moral judgments. His comment, however, that "the sabbath was made for man and not man for the sabbath; the law was made for man and not man for the law" shifted the emphasis away from observing the law for the law's sake and evaluating law as it affects people's lives for good or evil, and that is revolutionary. Following the first approach would insist on people observing the law regardless of how much harm it may cause on occasion. Hardly a generation ago, divorce was forbidden. There were no exceptions. That was the law. People accepted it and made the best of it, though living with a person who was violently abusive destroyed many people's lives. Divorce also occasions much tragedy. How to solve the problem in depth demands an ongoing effort, but to do nothing and ignore the damage is irresponsible.

The same can be said of the celibacy laws in the Church. Celibacy is a requirement for ordination to the priesthood. Many men know in their hearts they have a call to the priesthood, and even though they sense that celibacy may not be possible, they suppress their need for love and replace their fear of the potential risks with hope and prayer because their call to the priesthood is so overpowering. They observe celibacy during the many years of study and for a number of years afterward. Then one day it strikes them. I cannot live this way. As the reason to suppress their need for love no longer provides the strong support it did, since they have reached their goal, they finally realize they do not have a genuine call to celibacy, and that realization is devastating. From that point on it becomes almost an impossibility to observe it. They try and struggle and pray, but nothing seems to help. The frustration and loneliness is a constant distraction from their priestly work and leads to the most frightful and dangerous depression. At that point, some resort to drinking. Others resort to various other escapes. Some whom I have counseled have seriously considered suicide. In their depression and frustration, they often treat people cruelly and do untold damage to souls. It is sad. Is this what Jesus would want? "Let him who can take it, take it," Jesus said with understanding. It has to be a considered judgment made by a mature person, not forced on someone too young to understand the consequences later on, when their personality matures and they realize with their best of efforts they cannot live that way without it destroying them. When one considers there are over a hundred thousand priests worldwide who have left the priesthood and married, it is obvious to any sensible person that something is wrong. They were not bad priests. Some of them were the best of priests. They must have felt a strong call to the priesthood. Eight to twelve years of intensive study is a good test of that. A caring, sensitive hierarchy, if they are good shepherds who love the sheep, and their fellow shepherds as well, and really value the priesthood, would be the first to realize that something is wrong. Most of the priests who have left were excellent priests, caring, learned, sensitive to people's pain and need, and prayerful as well. Clearly, the priesthood and celibacy are two separate vocations. Demanding one as a requisite for the other does not mean that the Holy Spirit is going to cooperate and give the grace for both. The damage that attitude has caused is obvious to anyone with an open mind. In a situation as tragic as this is for all of Christianity, the words of Jesus stand out clearer than ever; "The sabbath was made for man and not man for the sabbath. The law was made for man and not man for the law." Where there is a human need, the law must bend. You don't insist on a law when it destroys people's lives and occasions unbelievable scandal to so many good people, and tears the Church apart, and attracts so many sick people into the priesthood. Jesus' advice on celibacy is short and to the point; "Let him who can take it, take it." He Himself made it optional. Insistence on the observance of a law when it occasions so much human tragedy and scandal points out the wisdom of Jesus' philosophy. When talking of human need, it should be remembered that the good of society is part of that consideration because it involves the long-term good of the total community. The above examples of forming moral decisions based on love are not far-fetched. They are at the core of many problems in Christianity today.

People may object that one cannot make moral decisions based only on love. It becomes too subjective. That is true if a person wants pat, simple answers to every moral issue. But perfect objectivity in moral questions will never be possible. We are seeing that more than ever now, when our society is dealing with issues never faced before and for which there is no answer in the scriptures, and no universally accepted answers from theologians. Even in the best of cases there will be subjectivity in the solving of moral problems. Moralists choose as premises principles and quotations that subjectively appeal to them in the process of arriving at a decision, so different theologians will offer different solutions based on different premises. Life's situations in today's world are too complicated to be shrugged off by smug cut-and-dried, black and white answers. To demand it is to fly in the face of reality and lose credibility with intelligent, thoughtful people.

I have struggled for a long time over St. Augustine's decision, after he finally accepted Jesus, to send back to Africa his longtime lover, who had borne his children. He later on was to teach that love properly understood should be the guide to making proper moral decisions. I asked myself many times, was his decision to expel that woman from his life a decision based on love properly understood, or was it without compassion and just to satisfy his need for the rigid observance of law? Would Jesus have counseled Augustine to do such a thing? Significantly, unlike in the story of the woman caught in adultery, Jesus did not tell the woman at the well to give up the man she was living with. Where would she go, with no welfare, and after already having five husbands? But Augustine's newfound faith taught him that living with her was sinful, since they were not married. Then, why did he not marry her? Was it because it might impede him in furthering his career? Clearly, it did not fit in with the plans for his new lifestyle. I often wondered what happened to that woman. Was she in a position to support herself? Did he send her support? Did she have a caring, understanding family or friends to offer her support? Did his rejection of her destroy her life? What effect did it have on the children? Love, properly understood, must be the deciding factor in making moral decisions. Was that decision made from love properly understood? If, in the keeping of one law you destroy another human being or cause untold harm, is that what Jesus would want? Is that what God would want?

Jesus always taught the highest of ideals, particularly about marriage. Yet, when He went out of His way to meet the woman at the well, who had been married five times, and was now living with a man who was not her husband, His words spoke volumes. In calling the previous men in her life husbands, He seemingly acknowledged, though did not approve of, those marriages, and took pains to note she was not married to the man she was presently living with. On other occasions He makes a point to tell the person to avoid their particular sin. With this woman it is surprising that He does not tell her to give up living with the man. Maybe He did but it is not recorded. It would seem that if Jesus told her, the apostles would have made a note of that and would certainly have recorded it, especially since they took pains to note their shock at finding Jesus talking to the woman, though they did not dare to question Him about it.

If Jesus did not make an issue of the woman living with this man, it would tie in with Jesus' understanding of human situations. In those days there was no welfare, no government support for the poor. If a woman left her husband, where would she go, especially if she had no family. Here was a woman married five times. Who would want her? It is hard to imagine even her family wanting her. With no income and no support, would she just roam the streets? Jesus could see all the frightening prospects for a woman like that. Could anyone imagine the compassionate Jesus telling her to leave home? Could it be that God accepted the fact, not the ideal, but the real-life situation that she was living with a man she was not married to even after being married five times? Why did He choose to meet with that woman, with all her problems, unless there were lessons He was trying to teach through His treatment of her?

Maybe not definitive answers, but it has to make one think. The late chief justice Warren Burger made a profound remark one morning at a private prayer breakfast. We were talking about crime and sin, and justice, and the effects of a judge's decision in a criminal case. He commented that a good judge will be very circumspect when sentencing a person, because the sentence will affect not only the criminal but the criminal's family as well. When a judge issues a sentence, he is also sentencing the family even though they may be innocent. They pay a price, and their lives may be damaged irreparably. Moral decisions are similar to the decisions of a judge. They often affect not just the person, but others as well. These others must be considered in making a moral judgment. Love God, love your neighbor. On these two is based the whole law and the prophets. What would love dictate?

This is an unsettling approach to solving moral issues, but it is, whether we are willing to accept it or not, the approach Jesus laid down for us, and it does make sense. There is nothing sacred about a law, except insofar as it benefits people or harms people and their relationship with God.

The question arises, however, how do you learn to love in such a wise fashion that love can be trusted to make solid judgments in difficult situations?

That is not easy. I suppose when one is young, guidance is essential. Here a great burden is placed on parents and religious leaders who have the responsibility to instill moral principles and teach people how to live their faith. Theologians may have to develop a whole new set of moral principles grounded in love of God and neighbor rather than law. Clergy can then provide solid guidelines for their parishioners so they can substantiate their decisions based on love properly understood. In turn, the people can then provide solid guidance to their children. It takes patience and long hours of training and inspiring example to bring a child to the point where he or she is mature enough to make solid decisions, based not on fear or blind emotion, but on a mature sense of real love and concern. In the beginning this has to be difficult. But as children grow, their ability to understand true love matures and making a decision out of love can make a lot of sense. It just may make a big difference in the way people will approach sex. It is true, they might make mistakes, but do we not make terrible mistakes anyway in trying to interpret laws? Different moralists apply different principles to the same case and come up with differing answers. We must ultimately leave the judgment up to God.

The way we have taught morality to children in the past was to teach the Ten Commandments. What we really did was teach children how to avoid sin. Our country and, indeed, the Christian world is in a moral mess. The Commandments for the most part are negative, demanding the minimum requirement of law. Theoretically, a person could keep the Commandments for a lifetime and never do one good thing for another human being. You could see a person dying in the street and do nothing to help, and still not be breaking a Commandment. What is there inspiring about a law, a commandment?

Early one evening I was driving down a busy street in a heavy rain. I noticed a figure lying in the street, so I pulled over and got out of my car. An elderly woman was lying there hurt and unable to move. I covered her with my coat and signaled passing cars for help. At least forty cars slowed down, looked, and kept moving. I was wearing my clerical collar besides, which should have been an added incentive to help. None of those people did anything wrong. They broke no commandments. Some people live that way and never develop a sense of compassion, because they were trained just to keep the commandments and follow the law. I will never forget seeing a prominent Catholic presidential candidate on television denying the reality of poverty and homelessness in our country, and referring to the homeless as drunks, drug addicts, or too lazy to work. God deliver our country from such insensitive Pharisees.

Jesus' approach was different. His focus was not on sin. His approach was to teach love, love of God, and love of neighbor, and for Jesus everyone was neighbor. To a child of God, no one is a stranger. To love God and to love others means not an emotional feeling, but a spontaneous outpouring of goodness that flows from the intensity of our commitment to God, and an instinctive sense of how this God whom we have learned to love for His goodness would like us to act under these circumstances. In short, it means to care, to be concerned, to have genuine concern for God and for others, and for all God's creation. It is a positive thrust, not focusing a child's mind on sin and fighting sin, though that is important, but on introducing a child to God, and particularly to Jesus, at an early age, so that the warmth and beauty of that relationship can bring with it a joy and richness that will surround the soul with beautiful things and give it the strength to resist temptation as life becomes more complicated. It is a much healthier approach to life, and puts a responsibility on each of us to be caring, concerned people. It provides a strong incentive for keeping the Commandments, for wanting to be good, because Jesus, whom you have grown to love, is your best friend.

That is why in the only example Jesus gave of the last judgment, He did not use the Commandments as the basis for judgment. He said, "Come, blessed of my Father, into the kingdom prepared for you from the beginning of time. When I was hungry, you gave me food. When I was thirsty, you gave me drink. When I was naked, you clothed me. When I was sick you cared for me. . . ."

To teach a child to love God and have Jesus as a friend and a role model in the way He treated people is to give a child a wholly different approach to morality. The child will still value the Commandments, but will now aspire to ideals far beyond the mere minimum requirements of Commandments.

It was love of Jesus that inspired a little boy to befriend a retarded girl even though his classmates laughed at him. He was happy because, as he said, he knew it was what Jesus would want him to do. It was also his love of Jesus that prompted the same boy to help a troubled student with his homework so he could get a passing grade in a difficult subject, and to learn braille so he could correspond with a blind girl. It was love that prompted a five-year-old boy to quietly put enough money on a store counter to help pay for a girl's Christmas presents when the store clerk was going to take them back because she did not have enough money to pay for them. There was no obligation under the Commandments to do such things, but actions like these reflect the beautiful Jesus growing within a person.

I think one reason young people become disillusioned with religion is that so many clergy are obsessed with Commandments, and, like the religious leaders in Jesus' day, judge people coldly on how well they keep the Law without considering the pain and anguish people are suffering in the difficult situations they face in life. Young people see only too often the lack of compassion on the part of so many clergy.

Applying the principle of love as the guide to morality on a wider scale so that it embraces society itself opens the door to all kinds of possibilities. In the Middle Ages the Church did this in a remarkable way. Jesus' love inspired people to start orphanages, hospitals, far-flung systems of education. In A.D. 800, Charlemagne, emperor of the Holy Roman Empire, established a system of schools to educate all the children in the Christian world. Bishops conceived the idea of universities available to even the poor during a period which some historians call the Dark Ages. By the thirteenth century there were over twenty-seven universities all throughout Europe. At the University of Paris alone, there were fifty thousand students, a larger number than the normal population of the city of Paris itself. Only prison systems seemed to have remained barbaric, as they are in many places today. Vindictiveness has always been for some reason popular among Christians, even when Jesus was so insistent on forgiveness as a condition of our own forgiveness.

Theoretically, civilization should be inspired and molded by its devotion to religion. A civilization in which the majority of the people are Christian should have a code of law inspired by the ideals of Jesus. But for some reason the laws of Western civilization have to a great extent remained unaffected by the spirit of Jesus and we still exist under an ancient Roman code of law. Our penal system, to take one graphic example, is godless in the way it degrades human dignity. Punishment for crime and isolating criminals from society is necessary, but it does not give society the right to degrade itself by treating human beings like animals. A society that is truly Christian will never abandon hope for a person whom Jesus has redeemed. It is the responsibility of a Christian society to endlessly attempt to heal the wounds and injustices that have given rise to crime. Oppression and unjust social conditions breed violent and unjust responses from the oppressed. It is not that we do not have compassion for the victims. That springs naturally from our hearts, but forgiveness does not flow naturally. It is something we have to struggle to acquire if we are going to be sincere Christians.

A truly Christian society will continually ask itself; "What would Jesus expect of us as Christian legislators and judges?" None of the monstrous cruelties and injustices throughout Christian history performed in the name of religion would have ever happened if society and church leaders were inspired by a genuine spirit of the Christ, and were guided by the principle "How would love properly understood inspire us to act under these circumstances?"

Jesus' sensitivity to human need as the basis for evaluating law is the key to the proper understanding of law. Too often law is stressed as an end in itself as if there were an intrinsic value to law that demands its observance, even though it may have long since lost its relevance to real life. Law then becomes a religion, as it did for the scribes and Pharisees in Jesus' day. Observance of law became equated with holiness, and the quality of holiness was measured by the perfection of their observance. Many religious people today equate holiness with the observance of law. That is so sad.

Jesus ridiculed the religious leaders of His day for their enslavement to law as a purely mechanical exercise, disconnected from any true relationship with God. That is why He could prefer a repentant excommunicated, notorious sinner to a Pharisee who was flawless in observance of the law. The publican was at least in touch with his spirit, and beneath his shabby exterior craved a reconciliation and intimacy with God. The Pharisee was smug in his self-righteousness and had no real feeling for God. This provides us with a surprising insight into the mind of God. For so long we were taught that God is a God of law, almost paranoid about our observance of law. Here we see Jesus, the true reflection of God, focusing more on interior dispositions than on the exact external observance. Not that observance of law was not important, but that what was really important to God was the orientation and direction of a person's life. It is what is inside a person that gives value to that person in God's eyes. If a person has nothing noble within, external observance of law will not bestow nobility. That kind of goodness is just a shell. Longing for God and compassion for others was of prime importance to God. This would naturally manifest itself in respect for God and respect for our neighbor's rights, which would lead to an even more stable observance of law, because it is grounded in the powerful motive of love.

Jesus could not have made our relationship with God more simple. He created us to become His children. He placed us in the midst of a magnificent creation and asks only that we love Him and love and respect other human creatures, and treat all His creatures with respect and gratitude. He gave us a Church to keep His message alive and interpret that message in the ever-changing human conditions until the end of time. He intended His Church to be a gentle guide and a vehicle for His sacramental life to His children. It should not be harsh or domineering. It should be a gentle shepherd and guide like Jesus always was with people, never overbearing or repressive. Judgment and punishment God reserved for Himself.

This is the paradox of Jesus' life. He is God. He stands for goodness and righteousness. He preaches always, in season and out of season, only the highest of ideals, even finding fault with the scribes and Pharisees, as strict as they were, for having weakened the sacred marriage contract. He then proceeded to reinstate it to its pristine integrity. He always had before His mind the vision of the way things should be and the way people should live. On preaching the ideals of goodness and integrity He never wavered or compromised.

Pondering this, one cannot but be stunned at seeing Jesus so casual and accepting of the common people, the rough, crude masses, whose lives were so far removed from the ideals He cherished and preached. And the gentle way He treats them shows not an approval, but an understanding of the frailty of human nature. So many religious leaders, conscious of their righteousness as the custodians of morality, rarely miss a chance to show their disdain for persons who are not married properly. We censure them and cut them off from Jesus. This is so strange, because we have been witnessing Christians in Africa and Northern Ireland and the former Yugoslavia slaughtering one another and we do not cut them off from

Jesus or from the life of the Church. It makes one wonder why we are so severe with people whose only mistake is that they remarried without the Church's approval. It is so unlike Jesus, who was always reaching out to embrace sinners, to carry them back home. And after carrying them back home, can we imagine Him telling them they could not sit at the table and eat with nice people?

Seeing this in Jesus gives rare insight into His attitude toward human spirituality. There seems to be an earthiness in Jesus' concept of spirituality. Spiritual books have in the past stripped the earthiness from spirituality and put it out of reach of ordinary frail humans. The fact that the Church rarely canonizes simple lay people or married people shows graphically that we do not consider their spirituality as worth imitating. Seeing Jesus and His acceptance of people where they are at and accepting the hidden goodness of the woman at the well, and the goodness deep within the prostitute in Simon the Pharisee's house, speaks volumes about Jesus' comfort with the very earthy spirituality He found in common people walking the streets. And He never ceases to hold up for admiration the humility and contrition and unseen goodness in people like the Good Samaritan or the publican in the temple, or the Roman official who pleaded for his servant's life. He could have the nerve to say to the scribes and Pharisees that prostitutes and public sinners would get into heaven before they would, which must have scalded them like boiling oil. What He was saying so clearly was that He could find goodness where they could see only sin and human weakness, while at the same time He had a hard time seeing goodness in them because He could see no goodness in their hearts, only obsession with law and the traditions of the ancients.

CHAPTER 5

JESUS' INTIMACY
WITH HIS FATHER

ALTHOUGH WE KNOW JESUS was the living reflection of God, the very Word of God, we still are deeply touched by the tenderness of the relationship between the Father and the Son. As soon as Jesus began His public life, His Father announces, "This is my beloved Son, in whom I am well pleased." During the course of His life, Jesus over and again proclaimed, "I and the Father are one."

When did Jesus come to a realization of who He was? Of who His Father was? Some say it dawned on Him only gradually when He was an adult. I cannot understand why scholars have a problem with Jesus knowing who He was, or who His Father was. I have never had a problem with this, even as a young boy. I would be more confused if He did not know who He was. I knew, even as an infant, who my father was. At twelve years old Jesus certainly gives a strong indication that

He knew His Father. "Did you not know that I must be about my Father's work?" He already was conscious of the fact that His Father had an important mission for Him to accomplish. Champing at the bit, as soon as He was legally declared an adult, He took His newfound status seriously, and entered the teaching chambers of the scribes and those learned in the law, and became deeply involved in their convoluted discussions, impressing them with His uncanny knowledge and understanding of arcane passages of scripture, even passages they found difficult to understand.

I think the reason I find it difficult to understand why some scripture scholars question whether Jesus knew who He was and Who His Father was is that I felt such a closeness to God as a young child, and all I had was a human mind. Since Jesus shared the divine intelligence with His Father, it was not something He could turn off and on like a light switch. With His divine understanding He had to have an extraordinary awareness of Himself and His intimacy with His Father. How can a person not be aware of his or her own intelligence, and know its potential? Or conscious of who he or she is? Jesus had a divine intelligence as well as a human intelligence. How could He stop His divine intelligence from thinking and from enlightening His human mind? It does not make sense.

What was Jesus' relationship with His Father? His inner life was so intimately bound up with His Father's will, it is easy to see why it was the focus of His whole ministry. "What does my Father want?" was His constant preoccupation. It was not that He could not make up His mind, or did not know what to do. He and His Father had long before decided what was necessary to bring about the ransoming of the human family, which for some unfathomable reason was so precious to God.

As our model, Jesus was also setting before us the example of how we could be focused on His Father's will and how we could approach problems in our own lives. God and His interests should be considered in our decisions.

From the start, Jesus wanted to share His Father with His new friends. "Let your light shine before others, so they may see your good works and glorify your Father in heaven." "Be like your heavenly Father in the perfect way He loves, and in His forgiveness. He causes the sun to shine on the good and the evil, and the rain to fall on the just and unjust." When you are worried and anxious, "Do not be afraid, your heavenly Father knows what you need. See, He takes care of the birds of the air; you are worth more than all the birds of the air." "If you need something, ask your heavenly Father, He will grant it to you, but be persistent; and if you ask in my name, He will surely grant it to you." "Everyone who acknowledges me before others I will acknowledge before my Father in heaven."

"I praise you, Father, Lord of heaven and earth, because you have revealed to little ones what you have kept hidden from the learned and the clever. But that is the way you are, Father." It is remarkable the way Jesus drew His followers into His own relationship with His Father. This was totally foreign to the Jewish way of relating to God. God often through the prophets referred to Himself as the Groom and to the nation of Israel as His bride, but intimacy with individuals was unheard of. Calling God "Father" was unthinkable and still is for Jewish people, as I was told very pointedly by a rabbi on one occasion, when I referred to God as Father while saying a public prayer. There is an awesome majesty surrounding God that should not be violated by placing ourselves on an intimate level with Him, I was told.

Jesus knew people were afraid of His Father. They had been brought up to look upon Yahweh as the frightful, awesome Being who omnipotence controlled their lives and watched their every violation of the Law. Knowing these people were functioning at a childlike level, He told them stories about His Father, stories that would help them realize that the God they knew was not what His Father was really like. One day He told the story about two sons.

"A man had two sons. The younger son said to his father, "Father, give me my share of the inheritance." And he divided his possessions between them. And not many days later, the younger son gathered up all his wealth and took his journey into a far country, where he squandered his fortune in loose living. When he had spent it all, there came a famine over that country, and he began to suffer want. He went and attached himself to one of the citizens of that country, who sent him to work on his pig farm, feeding pigs. He longed to fill his belly with the pods the swine were eating, but no one offered them to him.

"He finally came to his senses and said to himself, 'How many hired hands in my father's house have bread in abundance, while I am perishing with hunger! I will return to my father and say to him, Father, I have sinned against heaven and before you. I am no longer worthy to be called your son. Take me in as one of your hired hands.' So, he returned to his father.

"While he was still a long way off, his father saw him, was moved with compassion, and ran out to meet him. He hugged him and kissed him. The son said to him, 'Father, I have sinned against heaven and before you. I am no longer worthy to be called your son.' But the father said to his servants, 'Fetch

74

quickly the best robe and put it on him, and give him a ring for his finger and sandals for his feet; and bring out the fattened calf and kill it, and let us eat and celebrate; because this my son was dead, and has come back to life. He was lost and is found.' And they began to celebrate.''

This story has always been referred to as the story of the prodigal son, but in reality it reveals more about the father. In describing the father in this way, Jesus is telling us about His Father, what His Father is really like. It is a shocking revelation of the superabundance of the Father's love, a love that is so far beyond our comprehension, that what Jesus is telling us makes the Father almost look ridiculous. ''But if you really want to know what God is like. He is like the father I have just told you about. You will never be able to understand the immensity of His love. So do not be afraid of Him.''

Read the story carefully, and you will see it is the father who is prodigal, distributing his riches with such extravagance. What reasonable father would treat children that way, especially knowing what his children are like? But this father does. And when the boy comes home after living a dissolute life, the father, who had been day and night scanning the horizon, finally spots him in the distance and runs out to greet him, smothering the young man with love and affection. To our way of thinking it doesn't even make sense. No earthly father would act that way (maybe a mother, but not a father), especially without at least saying, ''Well, kid, did you learn your lesson?'' But not this father. He cannot wait to shower him with love; so happy is he that his son has returned.

I think we have to reconsider this whole story. The prodigal son is not the unusual sinner. The prodigal son stands for every one of us. God lavishly distributes His riches to each of us in great abundance. We have talents and resources beyond measure. It is a rare person who uses these gifts for God. We use them for ourselves and hoard them for our loved ones. Others can go wanting before our eyes, and it rarely bothers us. We may give some of the scraps to God, but not terribly much. We feel we hardly have enough to give anything away. We must save for bad times. But somewhere along the way, tragedy strikes and we come running back to God, desperately pleading for God to help us and heal the terrible pain we are experiencing. And God does. No questions asked, no impossible demands, just tenderness and forgiveness. God is so happy we have finally come back to His love. How long lasting is our change of heart?

I know it all sounds ridiculous and totally unrealistic. But Jesus is telling the story, not me. And it is the story about an unbelievable kind of love His Father has for His children. Maybe we haven't fully understood the limitlessness of God's love. Maybe His love for us is so great, it is incomprehensible. Rigid people who are accustomed to a rigid, inflexible God will scoff at such a thought, but it is clear what Jesus is telling us about His Father. Whether we like God to be that way or not, it is, as Jesus demonstrates, the way He is. The other son is the rigid, legalistic Pharisee who prides himself on his fidelity to all his father's commands, and in the fact that he has never done wrong. He is angry and resentful because his father so readily forgives the other son and, without even demanding an apology, celebrates his return. It is the mystery of God's love which we will never be able to fathom because it is so far beyond the way we think and feel. We feel comfortable when we can squeeze God within the limits of our own paltry human love, and see Him responding the way we respond to situations. We would like God to be vindictive and punishing to accommodate our anger and need for revenge. We would like God to carry out our desires for the vindication of justice.

Jesus reveals to us a God who is wholly different from that God, and from all the gods the world had ever known. It was the God whom Jesus knew intimately. We get rare glimpses into the tenderness of Jesus' own relationship with His Father. When we do, it is so touching. How often we see Jesus going off into the hills as evening approaches to spend the night in prayer, communing with His Father. How we would love to see Jesus at prayer, to understand how He prayed, to catch just a glimpse of the ecstasy of that beautiful love between the Father and the Son, whose love was so sublime and so far from anything we as humans could ever perceive. How did He pray? It had to be different from the way we pray. We pray without seeing or hearing, except with the eyes and ears of faith. Jesus saw God. He heard Him speak to Him. It was intense and intimate. When the apostles asked Him one day, "Lord, how come you do not teach us how to pray the way John teaches his disciples how to pray?" Jesus' answer was surprising. "When you pray, go to your room and lock your door and pray to your heavenly Father in secret. He who knows what is secret will listen to you." Surprising, for two reasons. First, it strongly indicates Jesus did not pray with the apostles. One would think that when they were on long missionary journeys, sitting around a campfire at night, just chatting and making small talk, and joking about priests and Pharisees, Jesus would have said to them as the embers were burning low, "Let's get serious, fellows; let's spend some time praying!" Apparently, He never did that, so we find the apostles asking Him, "How come?" Secondly, Jesus was a prayerful person and thought nothing of talking to His Father out loud at times, as if He were standing right next to Him.

When we see Jesus going off into the hills at night to pray, it seems to show that for Jesus, prayer was something so intimate and personal that He had to be by Himself, away from everyone, in order to properly communicate with His Father. He required extended quiet time to pour out His heart to Him, and to listen to His response. We can easily picture Him in the hills outside Capharnaum or wherever, kneeling down, sitting back on His heels, resting His hands in His lap, closing His eyes, and all of heaven opening before His mind as He enters His Father's presence.

"Father, I am so glad to be with you tonight. I have so much to tell you. When I began my mission, Father, people flocked to me. They were impressed with the healings and the comfort I gave them. They were also touched by my words. I could tell. I watched their faces when I spoke and I saw tears in their eyes, especially when I talked about You, Father. They seemed surprised when I said You were kind and compassionate, and understanding of their weaknesses, and the heavy burdens they carry. The crowds kept growing each day. Lately, however, things are changing, Father. When I speak I notice a questioning look on many faces, as if they do not really believe. When I talk about the kingdom of heaven, they think of David's kingdom and battles with Roman legions. I know they were hoping I was their Messiah, and would one day declare myself and lead them in battle. Now they realize I am not interested in their worldly dreams, or their thousand years of material prosperity. When I talk about storing up treasures in heaven, they think of gold and silver pieces and money in banks. They look at me lately with almost a sadness in their eyes. The other day, Father, I tried to prepare them for my sharing with them our life. I multiplied the loaves and fishes and fed them miraculously. They were impressed, Father. In fact, they wanted to take me by force and make me king. Judas was all ready to furnish the crown. But I escaped and fled up into the hills. I sent the apostles across the lake, so they could get away from them. I know you know all these things, Father, but I have to share them with you, and tell you all about what I am going through. I have to do it this way because I am human and I feel a need to share with someone I love.

"When I met the same crowd the next day on the other shore, I challenged them to look more deeply into themselves. I promised them my own life as the food of their souls. When I told them I would give them my flesh as real food, they looked at me in amazement and could not believe what they had heard. When they questioned me, I repeated in even stronger words that I meant what I said. 'Unless you eat my flesh and drink my blood, you cannot have life in you.' They grunted, 'This is a hard saying, who can accept it?' Then they turned and walked away. Judas' faith also crumbled that day, and I could see evil entering into him as his worldly dreams were shattered.

"I also noticed, Father, that recently Sadducees and Herodians have been teaming up with the Pharisees. They had always been the bitterest of enemies. Now they are cozy with one another. I know that they are plotting to destroy me. I can see it coming. I am afraid, Father. I know I should not be, but I have laid down the shield of my divinity, and I am vulnerable. I am really frightened. I can see where it is all leading. The crowds are getting thinner, too, as the people can see the authorities are not happy with me, or with what I have to say.

The people are afraid of the priests and their leaders, and are shunning me, except to bring their sick and crippled and their dying. I cure them all, Father, even though I know so many of them are too frightened to make a commitment to me for fear of being punished by the priests.

"Father, when I began my mission, I had so many dreams, so many things I wanted to accomplish for You. I thought I understood human nature, and would sway the people to come back to you. But it is not working that way. It is not that easy. They listen only halfheartedly. I am too spiritual for them. They want a worldly kingdom; all I have to offer is your kingdom of truth and goodness and the promise that they will one day live with you forever in your home. I thought, Father, that I could bring everyone back into your love, and tear the whole world away from Satan and present it back to you, but I now realize I cannot do it. And I feel I have failed, Father. I never knew failure. Now I understand the pain humans experience when they fail, when they feel they have failed in their marriages, and failed in being able to support their families, and to protect their children from harm. I share their sense of failure. Oh, I know I have not really failed in what I intended to accomplish in coming here, to save the world through my suffering and death, but there were so many other things I wanted to accomplish for you, Father. Now I realize these things are beyond me. I cannot violate people's freedom and force them to do my bidding. Perhaps in time they will understand, but it will be long after I have left. I only wish I could have done more for you, Father. I cannot shake these bad feelings. I am frightened. Stay near me, Father. I know you are always near. Sometimes, I do not feel it. I can see so clearly the things that are about to take place in Jerusalem. I see it all happening so quickly. I know you are always with me, and I have the strength of your presence. You are my strength, Father. Help me, and be by my side now that the end is near. I need you more than ever. Also, Father, help my mother. She will bear the pain of everything I suffer. She is so good. You could not have given me a more beautiful person to be my mother. Surely, her heart will be pierced by the sword Simeon prophesied so long ago. She is so good and so innocent, and worries about me so much. She has been such a comfort to me all my life. Strengthen my apostles also, Father. They are so weak. Sometimes they worry me. They are so frightfully human, but their hearts are good. Help them through all this. And, Father, forgive Judas. I know what he is going to do. He is not a bad person, just so much in love with money and needs so much to be recognized as important. Good night, Father. My heart is bonded to your will. I am yours to use as you wish, but stay near me with your strength.''

I think that must have been the way Jesus prayed. In His human nature He felt the same emotions we feel. He could share our pain, our worry, our feelings of discouragement and failure, but He never lost trust in His Father's love and strength which He knew He could always count on. In that we could learn much from Him, knowing that no matter how dismal things may look, God's presence is not far from us. With God nearby, what is there to fear?

This sharing of His Father's intimacy with us is one of the most beautiful facets of the Good News. Never before had creatures been invited to draw this close to the awesome divinity. When people leave Jesus in search of a meaning to life in faraway places, they will never find anything so comforting and so strengthening of their spirit as this intimacy with God that

Jesus made possible for us. It is not a nebulous kind of emotional floating toward nothing, or even a poetic identification with nature. It is a real communication with the living God, a mystical intimacy with a God Who talks back without using words, a God Who touches our minds and hearts, gently guiding us toward our destiny. It is one of the rare gems of our faith.

CHAPTER 6

HIS LIFE AND IMAGE
WITHIN US

"I AM THE WAY, the Truth, and the Light. Come, follow me!" Jesus said. Ever since He spoke those words, His disciples scrambled to respond, some quickly, some slowly, each in their own way. The problem is that once Jesus left for home, no one knew the way from there on. He did not leave a map with detailed directions. Each one was left to his or her own resources to chop through the tangled jungle of life, trying in desperation to understand what Jesus expected. Thomas Merton wrote in *Thoughts in Solitude,* "My Lord God, I have no idea where I am going. I do not see the road ahead of me. I cannot know for certain where it will end. Nor do I really know myself, and the fact that I think that I am following your will does not actually mean I am doing so."

That is the great problem in the spiritual life. Once we finally reach a point in our life where we want to take God seriously and decide to follow Him, we don't know where to start. So many people decide, "Well, now I'll have to start being holy like so-and-so. She's really holy and if I'm going to be holy, I probably should be more like her. I really can't stand her, but she has a reputation for piety, so I guess that's the price I have to pay if I want to end up in the right place." We start out on an untraveled road in the dark. It is frightening, and so often we feel it has to be unpleasant if it is going to be right.

When I was a child, it was all so simple. I didn't worry about being holy or perfect. I lived each day looking for happiness whenever and wherever I could find it. For some reason, I happened to develop a friendship with Jesus. I don't know how it started. I don't know what sparked it. It just happened.

When I made my first Holy Communion, I felt deep down that that was really Jesus. Each day after that I would get up early and go to Mass before I went to school so I could be close to Jesus in the Eucharist.

For years I treasured this closeness. He was my good friend. When I hurt, I talked to Him. When I was happy, sometimes I would think of Him, but mostly when I felt alone. I don't know how much of it I related to my life. My relationship with God was simple. I tried to do what was right, but never tore myself apart when I failed. I certainly wasn't obsessed with being holy.

When I was fourteen I entered the seminary to study for the priesthood. I was determined I would become a saint. Being determined by nature, I knew I would let nothing get in my way. I decided I would observe to perfection all the rules of the seminary. We had to remain silent after night prayers until after breakfast in the morning. That was no problem. I just made up my mind I would do it, and I did, even though not many others did.

I tried to be perfect in everything—my homework, my classwork, my daily chores, my prayers, especially my play. I could not understand why others did not have the same attitude. For me holiness meant keeping the Commandments, the rules, and the discipline perfectly. It did not seem at all difficult. It was just a matter of doing what was right, but without realizing it, I had become a perfect little Pharisee. In the eyes of the other seminarians, I must have been thoroughly obnoxious.

A series of personal crises occurred at the time, during which everything crumbled inside. I became confused. I could no longer feel there was a God. That beautiful sense of Jesus' presence left me, never to come back. What had I done wrong? Was I just a terrible sinner unworthy of being close to God? It could not be, since I know I tried to do everything right. My inability to find an answer led me to search the scriptures and the writings of the medieval mystics, and the directories of spirituality for a way to holiness that made sense. I followed all the instructions laid down. They were time-tested and practical as well as profound in their psychology. But for me that didn't work either. I was only too conscious of my shortcomings and my sinfulness, which was the insurmountable obstacle to reaching the heights of perfection. At that point I really did give up. Not my faith, nor the vocation I had chosen. I had quietly, without letting myself know about it, given up the dream of becoming a saint.

Always, however, in the back of my mind was the nagging question; "If Jesus wants all of us to follow Him in holiness, and He calls us to be perfect as His heavenly Father, how does

He expect us to do this since He made us all so flawed?" I was sure God did not create all these beautiful, intelligent beings and call only a handful to be holy. It did not make sense. God was too intelligent and too efficient for that.

It wasn't until long after my ordination to the priesthood, many years later, and after seeing the complex ways God weaves intricate tapestries of people's lives, that I began to understand Jesus in greater depth than I did in just reading the scriptures and spiritual books. God is simple, all right, but His ways are more intricate than the human mind could even begin to comprehend. "Be simple as a dove, and sly as a fox," Jesus counseled us. I am sure He was describing Himself as well.

The other facet of Jesus' personality, His dedication to justice, at times frightened me. He so often presents an image of gentleness and compassion, but at times warns of the judgment to come. While being judged by the chief priests, He sharply warns them of the final judgment; "I say to you, on the last day you will see the Son of Man sitting at the right hand of the Power and coming upon the clouds of heaven." This was one of the rare times when Jesus held out the frightening prospect of the judgment for those who resisted the grace of the Holy Spirit. It was usually to the hard-hearted that He made these threats, as if to shock them into spiritual reality before it was too late. It is an interesting twist, but the only persons whom Jesus seems to warn of God's judgment are those who have been insensitive and uncompassionate toward their fellow human beings. They were almost always people who were fanatically protective of the religious structure, fighting fiercely to preserve the "traditions of the ancients" as Jesus put it, and were viciously judgmental of all others not in sympathy with their rigid, legalistic ideals. He could see they were not really interested in God, but only in the structure and the mechanics of religion, and used these as a weapon to judge and destroy people. These people drove Jesus almost to distraction. He was frustrated because He could not reach them. They considered themselves already righteous. He accused them of having eyes that see not and ears that hear not. Usually they were the religious leaders and their hangers-on who felt they had all the answers to religion, and looked upon the common people as ignorant and as beneath them. In Jesus' eyes they were the ones who were truly ignorant, for they failed to recognize the Messiah even though it was the one critical responsibility God entrusted to them. They were to introduce His Son to the people when He came. Now He was here and they failed to recognize Him.

Ordinarily, however, Jesus showed the gentle, compassionate side of His Personality, and almost always to the ordinary, simple people who knew they were not particularly holy. He was trying to woo them away from sin into a warm and loving relationship with His Father.

It was important for me to find the essential image of Jesus, the one that portrayed what God was really like, the one He Himself wanted to share with us. It was important because the image we have of Him would determine the path we take in following Him. If we have a clear image of Jesus, we at least know where to start. It is so easy to go wrong and make costly mistakes. So many of us view our relationship with a judgmental God as centered around law. Our approach to the spiritual life then becomes focused on law, on the rigid observance of the Commandments and on the practices of religion rather than on God and on goodness as the natural expression of the love that flows from within us. Even those who profess that faith alone saves so often center their spiritual life around the righteous observance of the law, and usually with the rigidity of Old Testament observance, as if they totally missed the spirit of Jesus. Not that observance of law is wrong, but it so often becomes a fixation, an obsession. It is the problem with the fundamentalist approach to religion, whether among Catholics, Protestant, Muslims, or Jews. There is an unhealthy obsession with law and with everyone else's moral health. It was the scribes' and Pharisees' mistake. They misunderstood God, and in misunderstanding Him, they failed to recognize Him when He came. As we grow along that path of legal righteousness, we become proficient in the refined observance of law. Our whole spiritual life becomes a life of detailed observance, with personal righteousness as the goal. Persons who choose that route attempt to perform every detail of their lives with exacting perfection. If you love God, keep the Commandments, so they try to keep them, all of them, all at once. They search their lives and their hearts and delve deep into their consciousness so as to better identify hidden breaches of law, all the while becoming ever more introspective and attentive to every thought and action, becoming, in the process, progressively more centered on self. In the end they find themselves fighting a thousand battles on a thousand different fronts, and realize that it is impossible to live that way. At that point many give up, some have breakdowns. Many marriages are destroyed because of that fanatical demanding that everything be done perfectly.

In reading the Gospels over and over, I noticed how attuned Jesus was to nature, pointing out so often how things in nature follow patterns of growth. How many times He uses examples of farmers and vinedressers, remarking how plants flourish according to their seasons, how things in nature wax and wane according to season. Everything in due time, everything in due season, He would say. It seemed He was hinting that there might be deeper messages in that staccatoed theme. After thinking about it, I decided to apply it to various life-forms.

Each plant has its own growth pattern. A tomato seed will germinate in seven or eight days, depending on conditions. A kernel of corn will germinate in about ten days. A cactus seed will germinate in 180 days. Each will grow to maturity and produce fruit in its own time, in due season. There is little anyone can do to speed up the process. Each has its own built-in time clock, "due time, due season." Animals also follow patterns of growth and behavior.

Applying that to ourselves as humans, we see something very interesting. We have a body and a soul. We have our physical life, our intellectual life, our emotional life, our psychological life, and our spiritual life. Our body develops through long, involved phases of growth. There is nothing we can do to speed up that process. It takes eighteen to twenty years for the body to grow to maturity. No matter what we do, we cannot accelerate it. Our intellectual life also follows a pattern that takes twenty to twenty-two years. Emotional maturity and psychological maturity seem to vary among individuals, but still develop through phases.

If this is true of our growth in these areas of our life, and of the growth of other living things, why should it not hold true for our spiritual life. This was a stupendous discovery for me. It was one of the hidden messages in the Good News, and explains why Jesus was so upset with the Pharisees' approach to spirituality. It was artificial and destructive of the joyful spontaneity God gave to each of us, and forced an artificial perfection from the outside, rendering impossible the natural process of spontaneous growth from within under the gentle guidance of the Holy Spirit. Discovering this also revealed to me the answer as to why Jesus was so patient with the apostles, and not only with the apostles, but with people in general, accepting them as they were at that point in their lives, allowing them to grow gradually from within as the Spirit gave the grace. It explains why people felt so comfortable in Jesus' presence. It explains why Jesus never put undue pressure on people to be something they were not as yet, because it was not the due season, the proper time. It explains why Peter could still curse and swear that he did not know Jesus only an hour after making his first Holy Communion at the Last Supper. Jesus apparently did not put extreme pressure on him to control his impulsive outbursts during all those years they were together. He knew he would in time, when he had *grown* to the point where it would happen naturally as an outflow of his inner spirituality. Just to stop for the sake of externals, or to create a better impression, would have had little meaning to Jesus. For Jesus, goodness had to flow from the heart. Then it had real meaning. Just suppressing for show what is really within us would not be impressive to Jesus, because He could see into the heart, as He could foresee Peter's cowardice ending in his denial long before it actually occurred. To suppress all our unruly impulses all at the same time before we have the inner strength and grace from God will only lead to a nervous breakdown. We just have to learn to have the humility to realize we are seriously flawed and patiently, prayerfully, wait for God's grace to strengthen us. This does not mean we should give free rein to unacceptable behavior. We still have to do our best to curb actions that are harmful to ourselves or others.

What is also difficult in following Jesus is that He did not spell out everything in detail as other religious reformers did. It was intentional. It was the only way He could preserve people's freedom to grow as love grows. Jesus focused on what lies in the heart. "You judge by what you see on the surface of people's lives, I judge by what I see in their hearts." And in telling His followers to love as He loved, it constrains us to continually deepen our intimacy with Him so we can understand Him and what He expects of us as His friends, and grow as love grows, naturally from within, without imposing on ourselves artificial imperatives from outside.

As a result, following Jesus and knowing what is expected will always be confusing, as walking in faith is destined to be. Jesus may have explained things more clearly to the apostles, as the writings of the early Fathers of the Church indicate, but even the apostles did not comprehend everything the way we would have desired.

St. Paul does tell us, however, that baptized followers of Jesus constitute His mystical body. As such, we are all members of that body, each with our own particular role to play in the Christian community and in the world around us. This also was a critical part of Jesus' message, that we are not isolated individuals on a planet way out in the middle of space. We were called to live in community, in a community where people care for one another. That is a tremendous departure from religion of the past and gives depth to Jesus' law of love, which places us in relationship with the community, where we find fulfillment of our calling as Jesus' followers. We are responsible for one another. We are our brother's and sister's keeper. St. Paul describes this community as a mystical body, with Jesus informing all the members through baptism in which He shares His very life, bonding each of us to one another as the soul informs every part of the human body. It is in this we find our vocation, filling a need and playing a part in the growth and health of the community. Living out that role is what God has called us to accomplish in our life. We still do not know in detail, however, what is expected of us, but we now at least know that we are to accomplish something special, something that no one else can do but ourselves. We have been fitted for that work by special gifts and in special ways, and our holiness is tied up with that unique calling. We will grow in our own personal holiness within the framework of that calling. As we fulfill our role and cooperate with God's grace, we gradually become more like Jesus, channeling His light and healing presence into the community. As His life grows within us through our Eucharist and our intimate prayer life, we learn to think His thoughts and feel His feelings and become more and more like Him. Imperceptively we are becoming, without even realizing it, a truly holy person, and the wonderful part of it is we do not even know it. We are being fashioned by the gentle hand of God into that unique kind of saint that God intended us to become. There may never be another saint like us, but that is what is so beautiful about God. Each of His creatures is special.

Another remarkable facet of God's mysterious grace is that it is this very imperfect and flawed clay of our humanness that forms the substance of our transformation. It is our failings and weaknesses, as humiliating as they are to us, that God uses to accomplish His wonders within us, and uses as the engine that drives us to become the instruments of His miracles of grace to others. We become holy working with what we have been given, and within the limitations built into our personalities. And that is all right with God. He knows what we have to work with. He made us. It doesn't bother Him that we have limitations, sometimes severe limitations, as long as we are *struggling* to be what we are able to be, and are sensitive to others' needs and pain. That is why Jesus appears always to be so casual with people, even enjoying their company, showing that He has no difficulty accepting them in their weakness. When we become conscious of our sinfulness and weakness, there is little of self left, and then God is able to work with us and use us. When we are convinced of our own inner strength and feel little need for help from anyone else, even God can do little with us. We feel we can attain our goals without Him. With that mentality, God cannot share His grace with us. We are not yet ready to accept it. We feel we do not need it.

Once, however, we realize our frailty and open our lives to God, it does not take long before God starts to work within us, and to use us to reach out to others. We meet others who are having similar experiences and find ourselves working with them on common projects which soon begin to have good effects on the community. We begin to understand how God uses each of us to bring together His family, each one sharing with others so that no one becomes holy in a vacuum. God will work in us in such a way that no one is self-sufficient, but each contributes his or her part in the accomplishment of a wonderful plan that benefits the whole community. You soon realize that the work of individuals, as beautiful as it is in itself, is related to highly complex plans God has for the local community, for the Church, and for the civilization itself. God's mind is vast, immense. His plans are not paltry, or limited to projects within parish boundaries. Fulfilling our role in the mystical body does not mean doing projects for the parish. God's mind is too big for that. His plans for us are vibrant and dynamic. The lives of each one of us, in many unknown ways, touch and weave in and through the lives of so many around us, and at times reach people in faraway places as God's masterpiece unfolds. In this masterpiece even evil is a necessary ingredient, drawing from the depths of each the courage and strength and heroism that lie, often hidden, in the recesses of our souls, and are often tapped only by the pain and suffering we undergo.

We can see in the community teachers, leaders, healers. Some speak in various languages. Others have the ability to interpret what was spoken. Some comfort by their words. Others strengthen by their inspiring example. Some are prophets. Others interpret prophecy. Some preside at the assembly and heal souls. Some administer the resources of the community. Each is different. Each will become holy in his or her own work. Each is a special creation and does not have the others' gifts. That is all right. It is the way God wanted it, so we will all need one another. It is the normal way for the Christian community to function, and sensitive spiritual leaders will recognize and utilize those gifts, so the lives of all can be enriched by the gifts of one another. As we exercise these special roles, we are at the same time growing in an ever-deepening awareness of God. As our relationship with God grows, unhealthy needs that used to weigh so heavily upon us fade and our inclinations to fulfill those needs all but disappear. We see our sins and imperfections diminish, and gradually fade away. That is the healthy way to grow spiritually. Each day we add our little colored fibers to the threads that are being woven into the tapestry of God's plan, not just for our little parish, not even just for the Church at large, but for the perfecting of the human family. This is so different from the self-centered pursuit of perfection in the observance of laws and regulations that now appears so sterile and so self-oriented, in which even prayer can become just God and me. This new approach is outgoing and joy-filled because it is centered around God and around others. Slowly, we grow, each day becoming more like Jesus in the way we think and feel and in the respect we show others, even beggars and so-called ne'er-do-wells, because we see so clearly God living in them. We quietly share their joy and their pain even though they are called strangers. I think it is our ability to feel people's pain and carry their pain in our own hearts that bonds us most closely to Jesus, as our souls resonate with His understanding and compassion. But I think it is also the most difficult part of being close to Jesus, carrying others', even strangers', pain. "I live, but now, not I, for Christ lives in me" is the way St. Paul so beautifully expressed it. But is it not an essential part of the process of living more and more in God, that as our love for Him deepens, the more keenly we sense the inner "feelings" of God.

This is the unique kind of spirituality that Jesus promised to those who accept Him as He shares with us the joy and beauty of His own inner life.

CHAPTER 7

THE GENTLE SHEPHERD

So often when we meet a good person, it is hard to accept that goodness at face value. In the back of our minds there are always the searching questions; "What's his angle? What's in it for him? What's he up to?" I think, perhaps, one of the striking things about Jesus was that He had no angle, and it did not take long for people to see that, and His simplicity, His innocence. One of the things that took me so long to understand was the lack of sincerity on the part of religious leaders. I had been taught from childhood that clergy were dedicated to God. When I became a religious, I was convinced that religious superiors and bishops were different from others and were totally interested in the things of God and in the spiritual welfare of the people in their charge. When I learned that that was not always true, it was painful to accept. True, I had worked and lived with many who were holy and dedicated, but there were many who were distracted by personal interests or political ambition, while priests who were not in their circle of friends were struggling and hurting from lack of appreciation and acceptance and from the realization that no one really cared.

When Jesus began His public life, I am sure people had the same questions about His sincerity. When they found out that He really was what He appeared to be, they were totally disarmed. It was this sincerity and simplicity of purpose that made Jesus so threatening to the religious authorities. There was no way to deal with Him but straightforwardly and honestly. This they could not do because they had too much to hide. Their lives were too devious. They had sacrificed their beautiful true selves and lost the simplicity so essential to being a good shepherd concerned only with the welfare of the sheep. Sheep are timid and need to see that simplicity in their shepherds. Recently, while speaking at a spirited diocesan convocation in Lansing, Michigan, I encountered a bishop who radiated that childlikeness Jesus talked about. What a beautiful man! It was so refreshing to meet him. He was just himself, no airs, no aura of self-importance that puts people at a distance. He had been a simple parish priest, and when made a bishop he maintained that same simplicity and concern about his people. He brought tears to my eyes. Finally, I thought, a true shepherd in whom there is no guile. I had become friends with several other bishops and archbishops who have that same genuine goodness and simplicity. Their kindness renewed my own spirit at a time when I felt sorely alone.

I mention these things because I think this is what people saw as different in Jesus. They could see that selflessness, that simplicity of vision, and His genuine concern for people, unlike the scribes and Pharisees, who paraded their superiority and self-importance, and were devious and politically motivated. Jesus had no airs. He was just Himself. He was poor and had nothing, and was content. He had one robe, which His mother had probably woven for Him, a seamless robe, the one the soldiers gambled for at the foot of the cross. Jesus said on one occasion, ''The birds of the air have their nests, the foxes have their dens, but the son of man has nowhere to lay His head.'' It was not a plea for sympathy, nor a subtle hint for people to give Him money. He was merely stating matter-of-factly that He had nothing and was content having nothing. That alone would put them at ease.

This, I think, explains why women were not afraid of Jesus and followed Him everywhere. It is an unusual phenomenon seeing mature women follow a leader through the streets and from town to town, especially in those days when men were not supposed to talk to women other than their wives, especially in public. And these were not just simple people. The wife of Herod's chief steward was one of Jesus' close companions. These felt comfortable with Him, and did not feel they were jeopardizing their reputations by traveling with Him and caring for Him.

People could see Jesus was not driven by personal need to accomplish great feats, or to achieve political status or a reputation for Himself. He was just Himself, and people knew He had no hidden agenda, and would in no way use them for selfish motives. They were relaxed with Him, and entrusted themselves to Him. Jesus' treatment of the rich young man who came to visit Him one day shows that same detachment from people and also His respect for their freedom to search out and choose their own goals. ''What must I do to be saved?" the young man asked Jesus. "Keep the Commandments," Jesus answered matter-of-factly. "But I have done that from my youth," the fellow replied, apparently disappointed. Then Jesus offered him an alternative, but it was only an option, since the man indicated he wanted to do something more with his life. "If you would be perfect, go sell what you have and give to the poor." Jesus put no demands on the man, just answered his question in a detached, almost disinterested way. Not that He did not care, but it shows his respect for people's freedom. In that little encounter, it is significant that Jesus knew the man was rich when he first approached Him. The fact that the man was rich was not a problem to Jesus. He knew he was a good man. And you think of the other rich people whom Jesus had no trouble accepting; Joseph of Arimathaea, in whose new tomb Jesus was buried. Mary and Martha and Lazarus were by no means poor. They were quite well to do. It seems Jesus treated wealth in the same way he looked upon any other gift of God or nature. Money is just another blessing to be used wisely and unselfishly. Talents are gifts. They, like money, can be abused. As we use our talents for God's benefit, as we help others, so we can use our money for God's benefit, in helping others. If you have been blessed with certain talents and resources, be grateful and use them wisely and share them generously with those who have little. Jesus does not expect more, nor does He demand more.

In this casual way Jesus had of treating people, they could see a certain earthiness, a certain identification with human beings, and a genuine enjoyment in being human. I often get the impression being human for Him was fun, and He enjoyed it as no other human being could. He liked who He was. He loved to watch the birds of the air, so free and so graceful, and the sly foxes coming out of their dens at twilight, slinking across a meadow, looking over their shoulder every few steps, and the simple doves, so vulnerable to attack from owls and hawks. He noted the varied colors in the sky as the sun was setting. You can picture Him swimming while taking a bath in the cool waters of the Jordan on a hot summer day, enjoying the pure sensuous relief from the heat, or just lying on the grass, looking up into the sky, daydreaming, or even floating in the salty waters of the Dead Sea, enjoying with His friends the strange phenomenon.

It does not take much reading of the Gospels to notice that Jesus is always walking, never riding a horse or a donkey, or in a wagon. He is always walking. I tried to calculate the number of miles Jesus walked during the three years of His public life. It was difficult to arrive at a figure with any certainty, but just traveling back and forth from Galilee to Judea, stopping off at villages along the way, it was over six thousand miles, not counting the ordinary walking He would do around town in the course of a day.

His appearance was also part of His message. Who He was and what He looked like spoke volumes. He had no home. Often He slept in the fields or on a hillside after spending hours in prayer. Occasionally, He stayed with friends, like Mary and Martha and Lazarus, but even when near their homes, He would still spend evenings sleeping in the grove of olive trees at the foot of Mount Olivet. That was why Judas knew where to lead the high priest's henchmen to arrest Him. It was a secret, quiet place where Jesus and the apostles spent many an evening.

On a morning after a night in the hills, He would reappear in the nearby village. What did He look like? Did He look fresh and neatly dressed? Where would He have found a place to wash, or shave, or brush His teeth, or even comb His hair? He probably was not well groomed. His hands and arms showed the toughness of a hardworking carpenter. Walking the long distances He did on His endless missionary journeys, and not finding restaurants along the way, He must have been slim, though strong and muscular. His features would have been swarthy, bronzed, from walking in the hot sun for hours, and sometimes days on end. His hair and beard were probably not nicely combed, since it is hard to imagine Jesus carrying a comb in His pocket or finding the facilities to shave regularly. His eyes must have riveted people's attention. Eyes, the mirror of the soul, express so much of what we are. When people looked into Jesus' eyes, what did they see? I suspect each person had the eerie feeling; "This man knows me. I can tell. I can see it in His eyes. When He looks at me, He is looking into the very depths of my soul. He seems to know my deepest secrets, and seems to be telling me, 'I know all about you. I know what happened yesterday. I know how bad you feel. I also know how you struggle to do what is right, and how you reach out to hurting people and in quiet ways help them. I want you to know I am your friend and I want you to be my friend. I love you. Do not be frightened; I love you just as you are. Do not become discouraged with yourself. Life is not easy. Remember you are only human, and can do only what God gives you the grace to do. In time my Father will give you the grace to be what He wants you to become, but only in His good time, so be patient and gentle with yourself. In the meantime, know that I love you and I will always be near you.' "

I think that is what people saw in Jesus' eyes, not a maudlin, sick, sentimental look, but a look that betrayed a depth of vision that cut through all the sham and camouflage, and saw into the heart of each one. The simple, ordinary people struggling to live, with their goodness and crippling weaknesses, drew from His heart understanding and compassion. The mean and the evil and the self-righteous drew from His soul searing anger and instant condemnation. The scribes and Pharisees got a taste of His laserlike vision and razor-sharp tongue, "Woe to you, scribes and Pharisees, white-washed tombs, so nice to look at on the outside, on the inside full of filth and dead men's bones."

God walked among His human friends as one of them, nothing apart, nothing different on the surface, just like everyone else, so no one, not even John the Baptizer, recognized Him at first. "Though He was in the form of God, He did not count equality with God a thing to be clung to, but emptied Himself, taking the form of a servant, being born in the likeness of men, and being in human form, He humbled Himself. . . ." (Phil. 2:6).

CHAPTER 8

GOD IN HIS OWN IMAGE

As HUMANS, WE FIND it impossible to break out of a human way of thinking. Consequently, when we think of God, it is difficult for us to consider God as He is, and we end up reducing Him, giving Him a sex, molding Him into an image we can understand. As a result, we make Him one of ourselves, with the same myopic human vision of life and the same views and values and hang-ups that condition us to respond to situations the way we do.

When it comes to Church matters and theology, it is natural to assume God views things in the same way we have theologically concluded things must be, thereby putting God's thinking within the same theological framework as our limited human vision. This is why fundamentalists of all religions consider their way of viewing God and religion as infallible, and all other viewpoints not in harmony with theirs as either suspect or heretical. It is more to satisfy a need for security, so they put their ideas into neat, carefully crafted packages with no loose ends and present them as religion. They multiply absolutes which they canonize, thereby reducing the areas in which people with other viewpoints are "allowed" to disagree without fear of censure. There are absolutes, it is true, because absolutes are metaphysical and psychological necessities, but we sometimes identify as absolutes values that are really relative because they are not imbedded in God's essence, or in nature's immutable laws. Jesus commands us to love. That is an absolute that knows of no exception. We are always obliged to love, and to make decisions that are prompted by real love and concern for the good of another. Take a man and woman who are not married in the eyes of a church even though legally married. However, they have five children who depend on an intact family for stability and sound psychological and emotional health and survival. A clergyman tells them they are living in sin and have no alternative but to either break up the relationship or live as brother and sister. (I have counseled well-meaning couples who have tried to do this after a clergyman told them they had to do it if they wanted to avoid sin.)

The proper question should be, since love is the real absolute as far as God is concerned, "What would love properly understood prompt the couple to do?" Then we consider the issues. We know that love is an absolute. Then we ask ourselves, "Is living in a legal relationship, though not recognized by a church, a relative or an absolute?" It is a very important value for numerous reasons, but is it really an absolute. Second marriages may not necessarily be against God's law if the couple knew their previous marriages were so flawed as to make them null. To break up the second relationship would cause severe psychological and emotional damage, especially to the children, since they depend on the healthy love their parents have for them and for each other. I could imagine a spiritually solid couple struggling with the problem, finally deciding, "No, I cannot and will not leave you. I have made a commitment to you and the children and that commitment is sacred. I have a responsibility to all of you. You need me and my love for many reasons; we belong to one another and are responsible for one another. We cannot in conscience tear these bonds apart, do irreparable damage to the children, and think we are pleasing God."

On the other hand, I have seen people who had broken up their marriage in the same circumstances, and saw the family fall apart and everyone's life, particularly, the children's, become destabilized, and develop serious personal problems, and felt as if they had done something heroic for God. It was the Pharisees' approach to religion that troubled Jesus because it put law before concern for people, and made void God's law of love to preserve their human laws.

For the scribes and Pharisees, the law was an absolute and they found it difficult to allow for exceptions, no matter how much their inflexibility hurt people. Their traditions and customs were immutable. This is why they faulted Jesus for healing on the sabbath. Jesus' lifestyle was free from the clutter of the law. He was an authentically free spirit who drove the Pharisees to distraction. As a result, the religious leaders failed to recognize Him. "How could He be the Messiah? He does not observe what our religion teaches us as sacred," they reasoned. "Our religion teaches 'God is One.' He says there are three persons in God. We were taught the sabbath is sacred. He ignores the sabbath prohibitions and flaunts His violations publicly, scandalizing the people, making a mockery of our religion. The dietary laws have been in force for hundreds of years; yet He ridicules them as nonsense, saying, 'It is not what goes into a man's mouth, but what comes out of it.' He justified David's giving the sacred showbread to his troops for lunch under the pretext that the law was made for man and not man for the law, and the sabbath was made for man and not man for the sabbath. Our religion has for centuries declared the Samaritans heretics and schismatics and forbade our people to associate with them. He passes through their territory on every occasion and visits with them, preaching to them that He is the Messiah, and that they are as acceptable to God as we are, which, of course, is heresy. He has said that the time is coming when people will worship neither in Jerusalem nor on Mount Garizim, but will worship God in their hearts and in the way they live. He undermines the very institution of our religion. That is destructive of people's faith and loyalty to their religion. How could He be the Messiah? No messiah would act or speak in such a way. The Messiah would of necessity be patriotic in every way, a veritable model of national and religious loyalty, and would certainly endorse our authority. After all, we are the teaching authority instituted by Yahweh Himself.''

One cannot help but wonder if Jesus' attitudes toward our Christian theology coincides with ours. Does He have the same theology we have? Fundamentalist Baptists feel that He would be at home only in their churches. Fundamentalist Catholics feel that Jesus would be comfortable only in Catholic churches. He certainly would not approve of heretics or of those who left the Church He Himself gave us. He certainly would not allow miracles to happen at the hands or through the prayers of

Protestants. That would be showing approval for their brand of religion, and Jesus certainly would never do that. Fundamentalists of other denominations have similar ideas. God, of necessity, has to think the way they think, because they are convinced they are right. Others who do not share their beliefs are wrong and certainly could not possibly be pleasing to God. In fact, they are a danger to others' faith, and it is reasonable to destroy such people or their reputations. That is the mentality that inspires inquisitions and witch-hunts, and would happen today if these kinds of people had their way. One prominent fundamentalist pastor was ostracized from his denomination and lost his congregation because he said it was possible for Catholics to be saved.

One evening, after I had finished speaking about Jesus, a woman approached me. She was on the verge of tears. She was a Catholic who had just come back from a pilgrimage to Medjugorje that had been organized by her pastor and a Southern Baptist minister. When they arrived at the shrine, her pastor offered Mass. When the Baptist minister came up to receive Communion, the pastor refused to give him Communion. "We were all horrified," she said. What would Jesus have done? Is that Jesus' theology? The theology of the Good Shepherd? The lady also mentioned that when the children at Medjugorje asked Mary what her Son thought of Protestants, her answer was "My Son looks upon all of you as one family. You are the ones who put up walls between yourselves."

Yes, it would be ideal if there were unity of doctrine among those who receive the Eucharist, but is that possible, or even something that Jesus would demand among people who are already baptized and committed to Him? At the Last Supper the apostles still did not know that Jesus was the divine Son of

God. They were not even sure Who He was, still, Jesus gave them their First Communion. I am sure they were not even fully aware of what that Communion really was. It took a long time for them to realize more fully the mystery of Jesus, and even that, only after His Resurrection, when they began to appreciate the implications of all He said and did.

And today, when we are so insistent on orthodoxy of belief as a requirement for receiving Communion, how many Catholics would pass the test? I always took our theology seriously and, even when I was pastor, I myself used to prepare the parents and the children for First Communion and Confirmation so I could be sure they had an exact understanding of just what was happening. I felt and still feel that that is important. And I am sure it is important to Jesus that His followers clearly understand all that He taught. I am also realistic enough to know that most Catholics do not have a clear understanding of what they should believe, or a clear understanding of even some important teachings of the Church. I know many Lutherans and Episcopalians who are more Catholic in their own personal theology than many Catholics who receive the Eucharist. I wonder how insistent Jesus would be today on theological orthodoxy. I do not know, but He placed few doctrinal demands on those who followed Him.

Compared to the scribes and Pharisees, Jesus did not seem to have the same sense of theological propriety they demanded. I wonder how He would view our insistence on doctrinal purity, not concerning what He taught us, but on our theological explanations. Would He recognize us as one family that does not get along? Or would He be upset because we have torn apart His family, and wandered off in a thousand different directions? What would He demand of us if we all wanted to respond to His prayer for unity and become one family again?

He was realistic and earthy in the way He viewed and accepted human beings. He took them where they were at, as if saying, "Okay, I know where you are, and where you're coming from. We can't do anything about that; it's too late. So let's just start fresh from where you are now and go on from here!" I rather suspect He might say, "Let's start working together and in time we will find ourselves one again."

I also wonder how Jesus views our combining celibacy with the call to the priesthood. The priesthood is sacred and the calling comes from God. Celibacy is beautiful when practiced freely. I have been a priest for almost forty-five years. I love the priesthood and I admire and honor a celibate priesthood, and hope that there will always exist in the Church priests who are truly celibate. But I have seen so much during my long life, and have seen the pain and the despair of priests who found out only too late that they could not live alone. They were called to the priesthood, and that call is so powerful, a man will subconsciously suppress many other needs to attain that goal. Once attained, the other needs start asserting themselves, and then the terrible realization, "Oh, my God, what is happening to me. I cannot live this way. The loneliness is driving me mad." The depression that ensues undermines the priest's ability to work, to think, to pray, and eventually even to function. And this is not self-pity or self-indulgence. It is a sad reality. To relieve the depression, they often distract themselves in ways that do not honor their priesthood. It is easy for a strong person to judge these persons harshly, but I have counseled them and I know many of them are good, holy men, well-disciplined and faithful to prayer, even when it is difficult for them to pray. Often I have been tempted to suggest they leave the priesthood, but I know they have a vocation. They are good priests and people know that and love them. It is clear to anyone without other interests that they do have a vocation. It is just as clear that they do not have a calling to celibacy. A sensitive Shepherd would be the first to recognize that something is wrong. It troubles me deeply that bishops don't stand up and fight for these good priests and allow them to be treated so unjustly. That is one of the greatest injustices in the Church today, the way the Church treats priests whose only sin is that they married. It would seem obvious, especially when there are over one hundred thousand priests in this situation that perhaps there are two callings, and the Holy Spirit is free to give the calling to the priesthood to whomever He chooses, and if He chooses to give that person the call to celibacy, that is beautiful. If the Holy Spirit chooses not to give that person the call to celibacy, it is critical that we respect the will of the Holy Spirit, otherwise we run the risk of destroying the priesthood. When we see an unusual number of shepherds who are not kind to the sheep and deeply wound the sheep, and who live an unhealthy lifestyle, it must break the heart of the Good Shepherd. Perhaps we are attracting many of the wrong types of people into the priesthood by not listening and observing how the Holy Spirit is working in the souls of people. Jesus did make a statement about celibacy. It was very simple. "Let him who can take it, take it." If we are really interested in the example of Jesus, He did call and appoint married men to be apostles, and even pope. I realize there are problems and scandals just as severe among married clergy of other denominations, but that is another issue. But if Jesus' own words, "Let him who can take it, take it," have any theological validity, and St. Paul's injunction too ("Men of proven virtue married only once"), it might be well to reevaluate our positions, lest we find ourselves opposing the Holy Spirit.

Getting to know the mind and heart of Jesus is important in sharpening the focus in our theological vision. It is important not just for the health of religion, but to soften the harshness of overzealous religious people who have occasioned witch-hunts and persecutions throughout history. It is a sickening indictment of religion that so many wars have been waged, so many pogroms initiated, so many attempts at character assassination made, so many good people attacked mean-spiritedly, all under the guise of being faithful to God and protecting His religion and the faith of simple people.

I wonder sometimes if God cares all that much how we define concepts that even at best will always fall short of perfection. Clarifying what we believe is important, though I would rather love the Eucharist than be able to define its mystery. But it is for all of us an imperative to make every effort to understand the mind of God in Jesus so our people can grow in the breadth and depth of God's love and understanding and expand the limited vision that has so often characterized religious people. In understanding the mind of Jesus maybe we would find that He would rather have us stand in awe and appreciate the mystery, say of the Eucharist, than try to explain it. Even with regard to the Blessed Virgin, I wonder if it isn't better to recognize her exalted position as the mother of Jesus and the Mother of God and cultivate a warm and tender love for her, rather than to invent new titles, which will only confuse many people and which only trained people will understand. I would rather concentrate on *loving* the Blessed

Mother instead of *defining* her titles, especially when it alien-
ates so many people of good will.

The proper exercise of teaching authority by the apostles
and their successors was a constant preoccupation of Jesus'.
After choosing the twelve, He sent them out to preach and
heal. They felt a deep sense of pride, and understandably so.
To be chosen by such a remarkable individual to go out and
represent Him to others, to be His ambassadors, was indeed an
honor. It did not, however, take long before each one began to
feel he was, perhaps, more important than the others. Jesus
overheard them one day arguing over this, and in a kindly way
tried to steer their thoughts into a different direction.

On one occasion, however, when they returned from a
missionary journey, they complained to Jesus that they had
come across a man casting out devils in His name and that they
forbade him to do such a thing, since he did not belong to
their group. It is easy to see their thinking. "Jesus specially
picked us to do this work. We have authority. Who is this
man? He has no authority to do these things. The nerve of him
to dare do things that only we have been chosen to do?" So
they silenced him.

"Do not forbid him," Jesus told them, "for he who is not
against you is for you." Even though Jesus set up an authority
to bring His message and healing to others, it did not mean
that He was thereby limiting Himself to channeling His love
and healing only through those specially chosen. This is something difficult for many people to comprehend, and explains
fundamentalists' conviction that only through their ministry
can people be saved, because only they are the chosen vehicles
of God's true message. What Jesus was really saying was "I

know I have chosen you to be my vessels of election, but that does not mean that I am not free to work through others. If I choose to channel my power through others, that is none of your business. I will use whomever I choose. You just do your work and be humble about it, and do not judge the spiritual health of anyone other than yourself.''

That religious elitism that Jesus saw emerging in the apostles troubled Him because the Pharisees flaunted that attitude so mercilessly. They knew they had been chosen by God to be the teachers of the chosen people. Even Jesus recognized their status as the magisterium. ''Do what the scribes and Pharisees tell you. They occupy the chair of Moses (their authority comes from God), but do not imitate them, because they are hypocrites.'' What an indictment of the men His Father had chosen and consecrated to teach His people! They had misused their authority and stripped the people of the joy and freedom God intended they should have and made religion an ''impossible burden.'' They had tight control even over people's thinking, and threatened God's punishment for disobedience and disloyalty.

Another example of the breadth of Jesus' understanding of who was part of His family is expressed in the way He embraced the Samaritans. They were excommunicated Jews. They had been ostracized centuries before when a pagan army had passed through their land. Many of the Samaritan women had married pagan soldiers. As punishment, the religious authorities in Jerusalem excommunicated the whole Samaritan nation, forbidding them ever again to worship at the temple in Jerusalem. Jews were forever forbidden to associate with Samaritans or have any contact with them. In 490 B.C., when the Judean nobility returned from exile and were rebuilding the temple in Jerusalem, the Samaritans sent a delegation to Jerusalem to offer their assistance. They were insulted and turned away. Since then the bitterest hatred existed on the part of Jews and Galileans against the Samaritans, and vice versa.

Now look at how Jesus responded to this situation. Although the religious authorities had forbidden anyone to associate with Samaritans, Jesus went through Samaritan territory every chance He got, and befriended them.

The story of the Good Samaritan is relevant here. When Jesus told the story of the excommunicated Samaritan doing the kind deed to the hapless traveler, He was clearly showing that this Samaritan, who belonged to a group of people excommunicated by the Jews, was not excommunicated by God, but was being held up as a model by God.

If we are going to take Jesus seriously, we have to examine all the factors in the Gospel stories. First of all, the religion of the Jews was the religion given to them by God. Really, only God can give people a religion and tell people how He wants them to worship Him. In Jesus' day the Jewish religion was the true religion. The scribes and Pharisees were the magisterium, the official teaching authority appointed by God. Under ordinary circumstances, Jesus would have endorsed and supported their authority. However, He recognized that they had departed from what God expected of them as religious leaders, and had severely damaged people's relationship with His Father, frequently cutting people off from God and driving them away by their harshness, and their rigid view of Judaism and themselves as the only ones acceptable to God. For them God's family was just those people born into Judaism. For

Gentile worshippers, there was a special court in the temple separated from Jewish worshippers.

The prophets, particularly Isaiah, tried to expand the vision of God's family, but was resisted, insisting God's family consisted only of those belonging to their race and religion.

Jesus' actions, and His words, showed clearly that God did not share this theology. His view of God's family was much broader than this narrow understanding. When Jesus told the story of the woman at the well and the Good Samaritan, He was hammering home His own feelings about who is acceptable to God, showing in unmistakable language whom God considered members of His family. The religious officials had excluded from their religion people who could not measure up to the ideals. "I am the Good Shepherd. I go out in search for the lost, the troubled, the bruised, and the hurting sheep. When I find them, I pick them up, place them on my shoulders, and carry them back home." "Back home, where they belong," Jesus is saying. So even though the leaders excommunicated the Samaritans, Jesus carefully and delicately showed that He accepted them as part of the family. He traveled through Samaria often and preached in their towns, showing He looked upon them as no different from other Jews, and as we know, Jesus limited His preaching only to the Jewish people. He directed the apostles later on to preach to the Gentiles.

This is particularly relevant today, when Christians separate themselves from one another using theological differences as the excuse, their reasoning being similar to that of the scribes and Pharisees, that their religion is the only one that is acceptable to God.

I know that this will always be a temptation for people who take their religion seriously, feeling that truth is one. There cannot be two versions of the truth.

One day I witnessed an accident. Later on I read five different accounts of the incident. Each one was right and precise in what they reported, but they expressed only those aspects of the accident that struck their eye at the time. Putting them all together gave a well-rounded account of what really happened. One person insisted that his version was right and the others' wrong. He made himself look so ridiculous.

People are so different, and as a priest I have come across so many people with lives so different from one another and so complex that I have learned not to judge what I see. I met an elderly Jewish man, an Orthodox Jew. He had just finished reading *Joshua* and asked to have lunch with me. We had a grand time. He loved his religion, but told me he really loved Jesus and treasured His image in his heart. "I think of Him all the time and try to be like Him. But what have our religions, my religion as well as yours, what have they done to that beautiful man?" The man was very old and not well. He died a few weeks later. I could not help but wonder if Jesus would not accept him as part of the family, even though he might not have known all the formalities for being accepted as a registered follower.

On another occasion, while Sr. Dorothy and I were giving talks in Switzerland, we met a vibrant, intelligent young lady and her husband. The very first time we met, one of us had mentioned we were giving a talk about Jesus. She was all ears, and eyes too. She spent the whole day with us, and when someone would ask about our way of looking at Jesus and we would respond at length, she would stop what she was doing and listen intently. As she learned more and more, it was like someone had set her on fire. I have never in my life seen the Spirit of God pounce on anyone the way the Holy Spirit did on that woman. Her whole personality was like a lightbulb that had just been turned on. Even her husband, who, like his wife, was Jewish, commented to our host a few days later, "I don't know what happened to Jennifer, but I have never seen her so happy and full of life and so peaceful. Whatever it was, it had to be wonderful. I am learning from her."

One evening when we were preparing for Eucharist, Jennifer asked, "Oh, can I be with Jesus too?" She attended with us. I could tell she was filled with the Holy Spirit. Her face glowed and even though at times her eyes were closed, she was radiant. I was surprised when told later that she had taken Communion, and those who saw her said she seemed like she was in ecstasy. I asked myself, would Jesus consider her part of the family even though she had not as yet gone through the formalities of initiation.

A Chinese man we had met while in China wrote the most beautiful letter saying he had just finished reading *Joshua*. "I love him and think of him all the time. He is always with me, and I imitate his ways of doing things and treating people. I also pray to God now every day. And I teach Joshua to my students. They love him too and want to be like him." Even though it may be years before this man can even find someone to introduce him to a community of Christians, would Jesus not consider him one of the family?

One cannot help but wonder what Jesus' response would be if He were standing in one of our churches today and Christians of various denominations approached Him. Would He embrace one group as His own and hold the others at a distance? The Church is the living extension of Jesus' presence throughout history, so people should have the same experience when they approach us as they would in approaching Jesus. Jesus was always the Good Shepherd, warmly welcoming all who came to Him. The Church should be no different.

CHAPTER 9

REBORN TO BE FREE

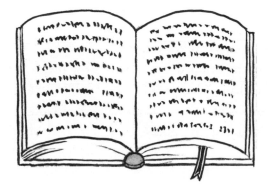

JESUS CERTAINLY DID NOT come down to earth just to be a nice man welcoming and healing and comforting people. He came for a purpose: to teach a message, and by His sufferings and death and Resurrection to redeem the human race.

In starting off His mission, the first thing He did was to announce His mission statement, as we all do these days. That statement was taken from Isaiah. "The spirit of the Lord is upon me, because he has anointed me to bring glad tidings to the poor. He has sent me to proclaim freedom to captives and recovery of sight to the blind, to let the oppressed go free, and to proclaim a year acceptable to the Lord."

Jesus came to reclaim His Father's children, to bring them Good News, to let them know that they are precious to God and that they are free. Freedom was the essential element of His glad tidings. Understanding that is critical to our understanding of Jesus' whole life, but also of the response He expects of us, namely to accept and act out that newly given freedom.

What does He mean by this freedom He came to give us? It had to be in reference to the circumstances in which He found Himself. The Jewish people had been set free centuries before, not only from their bondage in Egypt, but from their bondage to fearsome superstitious religions. Strangely, that freedom again had been stripped from them by their own religious leaders. They had stifled people's lives and restricted their free access to God. They made people afraid of God by using God as their instrument of punishment for noncompliance with their decrees. The people had been shackled by endless regulations and religious demands. They were no longer free. When Isaiah and Jesus spoke of freedom, it was not worldly freedom that concerned them, it was freedom of the spirit, freedom to enjoy their lives in the midst of God's beautiful creation, freedom as God's children to relate to their Father in heaven as any child is free to relate to its parents, and freedom to enjoy God and live without unreasonable interference from others. That is the only way that Jesus' concept of freedom makes sense. He "came to free us from the unbearable burden of the law that no human being could carry" was the way St. Paul expressed it.

It was not that Jesus did not recognize the need for religious authority to provide guidance, but He was extremely upset with how difficult religious leaders made people's lives with their senseless interference and their legalism. One would imagine religious leaders today would be supersensitive to this legalism, since Jesus made such an issue of it in His own day. A painful situation I have a difficult time understanding concerns a woman who is allergic to alcohol and also allergic to wheat. Since there is a good number of people with this problem, she asked if the priest could not also have available Communion made from another kind of flour, or at least a wine with no alcohol. A group of priests, canon lawyers, wrote to Rome for a decision. They were told it was against the law. So she is not able to receive the Eucharist, without which Jesus said we cannot have life. Can one imagine the pain that woman feels knowing she can never again receive the Eucharist. I cannot help but wonder what Jesus would say. Perhaps, "The law was made for man not man for the law. Where there is a human need, the law must bend. The Eucharist is of divine law; the ingredients are of merely ecclesiastical law. God's law should take precedence, lest we make void God's law to keep a human tradition."

The reason freedom of spirit is so important is that it is necessary for spiritual growth and development. Legalism interferes with God's ability to work with us. God has to be free to guide us in whatever way He chooses. If the Spirit of God is to inspire and guide us, we must be free to respond. But so often people are hampered by what parents and religious teachers told them what they could and could not do, rather than just helping them discern what God is attempting to tell them, and where He is attempting to lead them. When ministering this way, clergy can really be at their best and can affect people's lives in ways never dreamed.

Conflicts over freedom of the spirit and religious authority had taken place long before Jesus came. The problem the prophets encountered was over who had the right to teach the people. God had commissioned the chief priests and the scribes as the teaching authority in the Jewish religion. Their decisions were law, and violations were severely punished. At times, however, when the religious authorities were not carrying out their responsibilities, God called prophets and sent them to teach the people, often instructing them to preach from the temple itself. This infuriated the authorities. "We are the teachers of Israel. God Himself has appointed us for this office. You are nothing. How dare you teach the people?" That was the problem. The priests were insulted because someone else dared to do what they were ordained to do. "But God told me to deliver this message." That made no difference to the leaders, they still imprisoned and beat the prophets, killing most of them, and one of them, Zachariah, they killed right near the altar itself. Jesus accused the scribes and Pharisees of being guilty of the blood of the prophets because they had the same mentality and were doing the same thing their ancestors did to the prophets of long ago.

Theoretically, there should never be a conflict between freedom of the spirit and the authority of the Church, since God is the author of both. The two should be able to work together in a harmonious way that would make it possible for the Holy Spirit to accomplish what He wants in the Church, and what He wants to accomplish in each individual Christian, and in each individual human being, whether they have found Jesus or not.

It does not take very long, after we reach a point in our life where we are ready to turn our lives over to God, when God works closely with us, sharing His insights about ourselves and deepening our understanding of Himself and spiritual things. Our enthusiasm for our newfound life inspires us. We burst with energy and generosity, doing things for others, even family members, that we would never have thought of doing just a few days before.

Eventually, it dawns on us; "Maybe I can do something around the parish." So down to the pastor we go. "Reverend (or Father), I have all kinds of energy and ability which I would like to share with the parish. Is there anything I can do?"

And so often the response is "Our parish has everything the people need. We don't need anything else, thank you. If we need you, we'll call you." Sometimes the response is even more gruff. Those kinds of responses are devastating to people who are willing to be part of their community. Perhaps part of the problem is that we are inclined to view the community only in terms of parish, rather than the community at large in which we live and work and play. As needs in society change, the gifts God gives to people are to benefit not just parish, which is so restrictive. The Holy Spirit doesn't think in parish terms. The Holy Spirit's vision is wide and deep and far-reaching. When He calls people, He calls them for the community, so leaders in parishes can always find a need for people's gifts if they broaden their vision to include the community at large. In this way, we can always find room for everyone's gifts and talents or whatever they may have to offer. Unfortunately, I don't think seminaries train future clergy to think about the big picture.

We have always been taught that as members of the mystical body of Christ, each of us has a calling to something special in the community, some gift that God wants us to share with the others. If this is true, the community needs what each one has to give. What is also true is that each one has to be free to exercise what the Spirit is prompting. So often, however, the spirit is smothered when people are told that they are not needed. This is one of the most serious causes of dissatisfaction in our churches, and why so many leave. People know they have a gift to share, want so much to be needed, yet are made to feel not only not needed, but unwanted, or, worse, a nuisance. Why stay when you are not wanted, especially when someplace else is thrilled to have the benefit of your gifts.

St. Bernadette Soubirous had a prudent and courageous pastor who was sincere in trying to discern what God was trying to accomplish in her life. When he was certain the Blessed Mother was working through her, he was willing to defend her at great cost to himself. On the other hand, St. Joan of Arc's bishop, being politically motivated, refused to understand her and ended by agreeing to burn her alive as a witch. Only later did he realize he had made a terrible mistake and that she was really a blessed instrument of God. Out of guilt she was then canonized and a cathedral built in her honor.

As Jesus continued on His mission, He went from place to place accomplishing just what He said at Nazareth He was sent to accomplish, freeing people from their captivity to Satan, and from their bondage to the scribes' and Pharisees' brand of religion. What He was effectively doing was freeing people's minds so they could hear the voice of the Spirit clearly, free of the static created by the fear of God and His ever-impending punishments for nonobservance of religious laws. It is almost impossible for the soul to respond to the Spirit if it has been too frightened by religious upbringing to listen to anything other than what had been taught by clergy in childhood. Growth in the Spirit means ever-changing ideas, ever-deepening understanding of God and how God works in our lives and in the world. That means change. Fundamentalists in scripture, if they are too rigid, have a difficult time growing in their understanding of God and Jesus' message because they are frozen in the written word and afraid of change. It is the Spirit who gives lives and gives deeper meaning to the written word. It is the Spirit who inspires us to understand the written word ever more clearly and more profoundly. That means change, not contradiction to what is written, but a deepening awareness of the meaning of what is written.

When people are smothered with fear, the delicate voice of God's Spirit cannot be heard. We are afraid of it. It might lead us away from what we were taught. It never dawns on us that perhaps what we were taught could be built upon as we learn more. It was that same fear that initially gripped the prophets when God first called them. They were afraid to respond. It was all something new . . . and frightening, so different from what they were taught and the way they were brought up.

As Jesus continued His ministry, He traveled from village to village, freeing people—from their bondage to physical and mental illness, from their spiritual bondage to sin and to the powers of evil, from the bondage of evil spirits, and blindness of the eye and heart. Jesus really carried out what He declared His mission to be, a mission to set people free, and to declare a year sacred to the Lord, a Holy Year, not a 365-day year, but that short, blessed period of time Jesus spent among them, blessing their lives with His presence and His goodness.

CHAPTER 10

FREEDOM AND AUTHORITY

IF JESUS CAME TO set people free, He did not intend it to be at the expense of religious authority, which He knew was necessary to keep the memory of God's goodness and message alive. He also realized that He could not just preach His message to the air and declare it necessary for our salvation, then just leave it up to people to pass it on by word of mouth unprotected and uncared for. He knew it would be forever distorted and fragmented. That is why He chose the twelve. If He did not intend to set up some kind of structure, there would have been no reason to select the twelve or the seventy-two. It was to carry on His work when He left. He further defined their role by commissioning them to preach His message, first to the Jews, then, later, to the Gentiles. "Go out and preach the Good News to all the world, baptizing them in the name of the Father, and of the Son, and of the Holy

Spirit." "I will send you the Holy Spirit, who will bring back to your minds all that I have taught you." And again; "I will be with you until the end of time." Obviously the apostles would not be there until the end of time, so He must have been referring to those who would succeed them in the future. The apostles and their authority to teach is still with us.

In even a cursory glance at the Gospels you can see Jesus step by step setting up a mechanism to assure the faithful transmission of His message in its integrity. This makes good sense, because if He intended His message to be necessary for salvation, He had to guarantee its transmission in its integrity to all generations. So we see Him on one occasion, while He and the apostles were casually chatting one day, asking them the leading question, "Who do men say that I am?" Each came up with comments they had heard from friends and strangers alike. "Some say you are John the Baptizer, some say you are the prophet Elijah come back. Some say you are one of the prophets." "But who do you say that I am?" Then Simon blurted out in his characteristic blustery fashion, "You are the Christ, the Son of the Living God." To which Jesus responded, "Blessed are you, Simon, Son of John, because flesh and blood has not revealed this to you, but my Father in heaven."

That is an important passage. What Jesus is saying is that God gave Simon a revelation as to Jesus' identity. Then Jesus goes on to say, "And I say to you, Simon, 'You are Rock, and on this Rock I will build my church, my community of disciples. And the gates of the netherworld will not prevail against it. And I will give to you the keys of the kingdom of heaven. Whatever you bind on earth, I will bind in heaven; whatever you loose on earth, I will loose in heaven.' "

These passages are powerful statements. Jesus used words

that are very difficult to misunderstand, conferring upon the apostles, and Simon personally, a responsibility to pass on His message until the end of time. That's authority. In the last statement Jesus is telling Simon, whose name He has now changed to Rock, that His bearing witness to His true identity is the result of a direct revelation from God. It is interesting that it was not given to the others who were standing right there, but only to Simon, stating that His Father would guide and safeguard his teaching in a special way.

It is hard to look at those passages and not conclude that Jesus was promising to be with His community of believers forever and, in a special way, with those who would succeed the apostles in their ministry to teach and guide the community.

When we see throughout the Gospels the problem that Jesus had with the scribes and Pharisees' exercise of authority, you wonder what kind of authority Jesus had in mind for the apostles and those who were to succeed them. One day Jesus and the apostles are walking along, apparently across an open field. It seems Jesus is a bit ahead of the apostles, because they certainly would not be talking the way they were if they knew He was listening, which He really was. What they were talking about was who was the most important among them. You can easily imagine the conversation. James and John saying, "Face it, we got it made when He sets up the kingdom. After all, we are cousins, His mother and our mother are sisters. Our mother will make sure we get the first and second places in the kingdom."

You can imagine the others expressing why they should be the ones chosen for places of honor. You can almost hear Peter bellowing, "You guys can say all you want about being relatives and about blood being thicker than water, but look what the Lord said to me the other day, 'Blessed are you, Simon, Son of John. You are Rock and on this Rock I will build my church and the gates of hell will not prevail against it. And I give to you the keys of the kingdom of heaven. Whatever you bind on earth, I will bind in heaven; and whatever you loose on earth I will loose in heaven.' Top that!''

Trying to imagine the rest of the story, it seems as if Jesus slowed down so they could catch up, then said to them, "What were you talking about back there?" So delicate, so genteel, so kind in the way He suggested another model of authority. You can almost see Him saying it with tongue in cheek, yet seriously nonetheless. But what follows is important. "You know, important people of this world love to lord it over their subjects and make their importance felt. It cannot be that way with you. Whoever wishes to be first among you must be willing to be the servant of all the rest." What kind of authority is that? That was not the kind of authority the apostles had in mind. They wanted power. They wanted to enjoy their positions of authority. Jesus totally confused them. "Why does He have to be so different from everybody else? He's got it made if He would let Himself go and not be so humble. We will never be able to understand Him. He's so different.''

When you go through the Gospels again, you begin to see that Jesus did exercise authority, but it was a unique kind of authority. He had authority over demons and over people's illnesses. He healed, He consoled, He comforted, He raised the dead to life, He gave sight to the blind. That was power. That was authority. But most of all He taught with authority, not by threatening and doing violence to people's minds, but by the power of His word He made the truth clearer than any human could ever possibly do. What He did most of all, He taught by the beauty of His life and His example. His whole being and demeanor spoke with authority, and people listened and followed, so much so that the heavy-handed power and authority of the high priest himself was threatened and prompted the officials to demand that something be done about Jesus. That kind of authority was the kind of authority Jesus had in mind for His apostles, a gentle, kind authority that persuaded by the inherent power of the message itself. As powerful as Jesus was, He never bullied or used oppressive tactics to force people into submission. How beautiful and attractive Christianity would be if Christian leaders imitated Jesus' humility, gentleness, and courtesy in the exercise of authority. If someone in Jesus' group did not understand and found hard to accept something Jesus taught, can you imagine Jesus saying, "Leave, you are a heretic. You can no longer follow me." I am sure He would try to help this person understand and draw this person even closer to Himself.

With all that Jesus did to teach the apostles what authority meant, you cannot help but get the impression that toward the end of His life Jesus was still concerned that they did not understand how they were to exercise their role. So after the Last Supper, He rose from the table, took off His cloak, got a bowl of water and a towel, and got on His knees before the apostles, and to their horror and shame began to wash the feet of each one. They were never so humiliated. As He approached Peter, He could not find his feet. He had apparently slipped them up under himself. "Never, never, Lord! You will never wash my feet!" "All right, Peter. But if I do not wash your feet, you can have no part with me." "Well, if you feel that strongly about it, Lord, then wash my hands and my feet." "Peter, stop being such a clown. Put your feet out here."

Then, sitting back on His heels, throwing the towel over His arm and folding His hands in His lap, He looks up into the eyes of the apostles. "You call me Lord and Master, and rightly so, for so I am. But if I as Lord and Master can kneel and wash your feet, so you should be willing to wash the feet of one another." He was still trying to get across to the apostles what He meant by authority and how He intended they should exercise that authority when the time came, which was very soon.

Obviously, Jesus did not mean that they should physically wash the feet of the people, but that they should be willing to do menial things to be of service to the flock, and not rule like earthly potentates by issuing decrees and threatening dire punishments for noncompliance. And there is a practical side to Jesus' humble exercise of authority. Where there is love and humility on the part of authority, people naturally want to oblige. When Pope John XXIII was pope, many of my Jewish friends, and Protestant as well, said, "He's not just your pope, he's our pope too." They loved him. It is strange how people even not of our own religion want to feel accepting of the pope. When they find one who is Jesuslike, they rave about him. When popes become harsh and threatening and combative, they feel offended. They used to read what Pope John wrote and discuss it and talk about it in their churches and synagogues. It is strange how people not even of our religion want to feel close to the pope. When that authority is harsh, people walk the other way. I have seen more people leave the Church, and others with goodwill turn away from the Church because of the insensitive abuse of that authority than by the teachings of a marginal theologian whom the vast majority of people never heard of until they were punished.

Still Jesus did give authority to the apostles and to their successors, and Peter is still very much with us today. He will always be part of the heritage that Jesus gave us. And if we want to be faithful to Jesus, and to the scriptures, we have to take Peter seriously, and reevaluate our attitude toward Peter in our time.

While Jesus did establish a teaching authority to guarantee the faithful transmission of His message, He also gave His followers freedom to live under the guidance of the Holy Spirit. Since Jesus is the author of both, they cannot be contradictory but must be reconcilable. There should never be a real conflict if there is proper respect one for the other.

How do we exercise this beautiful freedom that Jesus gave us? First, it is important that we learn to understand ourselves, and that we take our faith seriously, and understand our faith in depth. There will be times when we find ourselves in difficult predicaments and must make a decision between seemingly impossible choices. And there are situations like that. A man owned a relatively large business. It was a good business but fell on hard times. By laying off a number of employees, he could ride out the storm and survive. After many sleepless nights, and much prayer and soul-searching, he had decided to lay off a certain number, so the company could stay viable. His pastor heard of what he intended to do. He met with him and told him it would be immoral to lay off all those people. Think of all the families it would hurt and the damage to all those people. Reluctantly, the man followed his clergyman's bidding. A year and a half later the company was forced to declare bankruptcy. All the employees lost their jobs.

Was it wise for the man to let the clergyman make his decision for him? There are many issues that arise in our lives where we have to decide between what religious leaders say we should do and what we think we should do. When we appear before God, we will have to answer for our own decisions. God gave us intelligence and free will to make decisions. We do not have the right to pass that responsibility on to anyone else no matter who that person is. We will be judged on what we ourselves thought we should do, not on what we were told we must do.

Yet there is an authority God gave to His Church. What is its role in our decision-making process? When we have a difficult decision to make, we naturally search our souls in prayer. If the problem involves complex issues, it is prudent to read extensively on the matter, and consult someone knowledgeable and whom we can trust to be honest and objective. If the Church has made a statement on the matter, it is important to read what has been said and accept it with respect. If we can honestly accept what has been said, then we can in good conscience use that in making our decision. If, however, we have a problem with that, or if the issue is more complex than what is covered in the Church's statement, then we are forced back on ourselves and our own resources to resolve the problem. God often guides us in these difficult matters when we pray with open minds and open hearts. After praying hard and searching our conscience, we then make whatever decision we judge we should make, and ask God for His help.

If events show that the decision turns out to have been the right one, thank God. If it proves to have been a mistake, well, our freedom and responsibility to make decisions also includes our right to make an honest mistake, which we then go about correcting. I think that is the only intelligent way for us to respect the freedom God gave us and the authority to teach which He gave to His Church.

When I first became pastor, I did a lot of soul-searching. After a few weeks, I had made my decision as to how I would carry out my responsibilities. I told the parishioners one weekend that I would let them administer their own community. I felt they were already working on projects and committees in the city, and some had their own businesses; it certainly would not be too much for them to operate a parish committee and carry out the decisions without my help. So I turned the parish over to them, telling them that I was not going to be their boss, telling them what to do.

We then set up the parish in a way the people could respond to the needs of the community. A number of committees was established, among them a finance committee, a religious education committee, a committee to work with the poor, a committee to work with the rich, a building and grounds committee, a committee to work with the elderly and shut-ins, a committee to visit the hospitals and do follow-up work later on, a committee to work with people being released from jail and who might need employment, a committee to work with the Protestant communities, a committee to work with our Jewish friends, who had become very close to us. There were other committees as well, for whatever the people felt was needed.

I did appoint the chairpersons of each committee, because I knew from experience that there can be too much politicking when the people elect officers for the parish, who are then subjected to pressure by those who elected them. I told the committees that since the community was not on the church grounds, I did not want them meeting in the church buildings. They were to meet in one another's homes. I would not be attending the meetings and they were to make whatever decisions they felt were needed and I would rarely veto what they decided. The next day the chairpersons were to report to me what they had decided. In the six years I was there, I never vetoed any of their decisions, though I did make suggestions which I felt would be helpful.

I was amazed at the maturity and conscientiousness of the people. They accomplished all kinds of remarkable things. The state had taken over the local synagogue to build a highway. The compensation they gave the Jewish people was not enough to rebuild their synagogue, so our parish council voted unanimously to start a fund-raising drive to rebuild the synagogue. The Jewish people were thrilled, though it turned out that they did not need the help, since some of their people decided to come up with what was needed. As the rabbi expressed it, some apples that were glued to the tree finally fell off. When the synagogue was constructed, the rabbi asked if I would speak at the dedication. This was an Orthodox synagogue. In my talk I mentioned how close our two communities had grown over the years, and I would love to see the day when I could become a member of their synagogue and still be pastor at Our Lady of Mount Carmel, and any of their people who felt so drawn could become a member of our parish and still be members in good standing of the synagogue. There followed a loud ovation. After the ceremony, two Orthodox rabbis approached me and said, "What a remarkable suggestion. There is no reason why it cannot work." And I meant what I said. I even went and made the proposal to the bishop, and then wrote up a paper and sent it to the Vatican's apostolic delegate in Washington, who gave it to the American Catholic Bishops' liaison person with the Jewish community. He did not see a problem with it, remarking that there was nothing contradictory in the proposal and that we have to start somewhere.

The parishioners also formed a beautiful relationship with a Lutheran community in the city. We did all kinds of things together, and celebrated liturgies together and talked both of our bishops into being willing to co-confirm the children in both of our parishes.

On Christmas Eve every year, Santa Claus would travel through the parish on a horse-drawn sleigh, with huge bagfuls of toys mostly donated by a beautiful Jewish couple, Emanuel and Rose Rosen. My cook, Lena Brignole, sewed the toy bags and made all the arrangements. It was so much fun. The streets in our little isolated section of the city were lined with little children and their parents or grandparents waiting eagerly for Santa Claus to come driving by in his sleigh. As he approached, the children started jumping up and down wildly, some singing "Jingle Bells," while others just screamed out "Santa Claus, Santa Claus," as the sleigh slid down the snow-covered street. I think the grandparents got more of a thrill out of it than even the kids. I guess no matter how old we are, there's still room for things like Santa Claus in our hearts.

Another heartwarming project the people got involved in was over choir robes. We had some thirty-five people in the choir. They decided they wanted robes. I asked where they were going to get the money for them. They told me half the women in the choir work at Joel and Florence Kaplan's dress factory, and they could ask Mr. Kaplan if they could use the machines after hours. As it turned out, not only did he let them use the machines, he gave them bolts of beautiful blue and gold cloth to make enough robes for the whole choir.

What a shock for me when I went out on the altar one Sunday morning and saw the choir dressed in beautiful blue and gold robes. They later asked if the Kaplans could be honorary members of the choir. I said, "Why honorary? They can join the choir if they like. Joel and Florence were thrilled. Even though I have been long gone from that parish, the Kaplans and the Rosens are still very dear friends.

Though I had turned the parish over to the parishioners, I soon realized I had more authority than most pastors who hold tight reins. The people were so respectful of my concerns that they did nothing that would embarrass or offend me in any way. Besides, I was totally free to provide spiritual guidance to the people, bring Jesus to other parts of the community, and accomplish much more than if I insisted on micromanaging the parish. It was for me a wonderful example of how respect for people's freedom and people's respect for the church's authority could work so beautifully and productively together, because the Holy Spirit was "allowed" to be free.

Sometimes decision-making involves other matters in which the Church may be more directly involved, as in the writings on sacred scripture and theology. These matters involve more than free will. They also involve the Church's right and obligation to teach and provide sound guidance for people.

These issues, as delicate as they may be, can also be resolved in a way that would honor Jesus. Sometimes theologians have used their licensed positions at a Church-sponsored university to propose ideas that are counter to the Church's stand on issues. That is unfortunate, because they contract to teach Catholic theology and precipitate a crisis when they misuse

137

their position. The religious authorities, then, have few options as to what they must do.

However, there are many solid theologians who have solid ideas, but suggest different approaches to understanding a teaching. Or they may suggest that Church authorities reevaluate some particular teaching. They are often holy persons who are not only sincere and loyal theologians, but are honestly sharing insights the Holy Spirit may have given them. Sometimes they are rudely treated by Church officials, and this is scandalous, and does much harm to the reputation of the Church. I will never forget when I was a young theology student in Washington. I attended a lecture at Catholic University. The lecturer was Fr. John Courtney Murray, and he proposed that the Church could work well within the framework of a democracy. The next week another theologian delivered a lecture ridiculing Fr. Murray's theory. Not long after Fr. Murray was silenced by Cardinal Ottaviani, the Prefect of the Holy Office (now the Congregation for the Doctrine of the Faith). When Vatican Council II was convened not many years later, Fr. Murray was invited as a theological expert and his ideas on the Church's working within a democracy were accepted as the official teaching of the Catholic Church. Why could he not have been treated courteously from the beginning.

One cannot help but wish that theologians at times were more sensitive to the ordinary people's faith when they propose ideas that are much different from the way people were taught about their faith. This can seriously damage people's simple faith. But also one cannot help but wish that officials in the Vatican charged with safeguarding the faith were more respectful of sincere people's intelligence and freedom. What is so wrong about sitting down like mature human beings and discussing difficult issues so they can be expressed in a way that is acceptable? It embarrasses the whole Church and other people of goodwill when authority is wielded in a way that is crude and unlike Jesus' sensitive manner.

Since the Holy Spirit is the author of human freedom and also the authority of the Church, it can be so beautiful when Church authorities and preachers and authors show respect for one another and try in a courteous and Christian manner to work toward a healthy resolution of difficult issues. There is no room for arrogance and mean-spiritedness in those who represent Jesus. It was one thing that troubled Jesus deeply before He died, and prompted Him to wash the apostles' feet to teach them humility and respect for the lowly members of the community.

CHAPTER 11

A GENTLE SAVIOR
BEARING GIFTS

THE APOCRYPHAL GOSPEL ACCORDING to Thomas and the Gospel on the childhood of Jesus contain many anecdotes about the boy Jesus, about His working with Joseph in the carpenter shop, and Mary teaching Him the scriptures, and a host of other interesting details of doubtful verity. Since Jesus came to earth to be "like us in all things but sin," we have to assume that He learned the same ways we do. No doubt His intellectual faculties were of the highest order, which made it possible for Him to grasp things quickly and not easily forget. Even at twelve years old He impressed the religious teachers in the temple with His grasp of scripture and His wisdom. Even today, looking back, one cannot but be impressed with Jesus' knowledge of the scriptures, and the facility with which He could quote them from memory, and use them with such extraordinary insight and skill in His almost daily confrontations with the scribes and Pharisees.

Scripture was an enriching part of not only His spiritual life but His everyday life. Not that He quoted scripture all day long, but since the secular life of the Jewish people was interwoven with the religious law, the Jews had to know scripture the way we know our traffic laws.

As filled with a sense of scripture as Jesus was, it is interesting that He never told His apostles to start preparing for additions to the scriptures, or to write a new scripture, or write down new mandates or practices. He never taught them the way His Father on Mount Sinai taught Moses, by issuing commandments and decrees to be passed on to future generations, or the way He spoke to the prophets when He wanted them to deliver messages to the people. When He gathered disciples around Him, He taught them, sometimes in parables, sometimes in plain language about healthy things that were good for people. Even in small groups with just friends, He told them about things with which He was familiar. He shared His life, which He wanted His followers to be a part of. It was intimate and personal. He told the people His Father wanted them to be His children and His friends. When Christianity put the trappings of royal courts into its structure, it made itself foreign to the mind and spirit of Jesus. Jesus knew He was King, but that was not what He wanted the people to see in Him. "Come to me, all you who are weary and heavily burdened, and I will refresh you, for I am meek and humble of heart." All Jesus wanted from people was their friendship, and for them to establish a warm relationship with His Father, "Call Him Abba, Father." (Abba really means "Daddy," or "Papa.") That shows how natural Jesus wanted our religion to be. The artificialities of religious structures seemed to mean little to Jesus. He wanted people to share His life and the life of His Father and the Holy Spirit. You do not set up a structure when you want to establish a friendship with someone. That has been the problem with religions. Officials design complicated religious structures which then become another way of life superimposed on people's ordinary normal way of living. That is why people often have a difficult time with religion. They feel they just cannot be themselves, but have to be something they are not, wear certain clothes, or let their hair grow a certain way, or not eat certain foods, or take oaths that do violence to their integrity, or believe contrary to what their intelligence tells them, or observe a host of required practices and customs and prayers. That is why Jesus' New Way was so shockingly beautiful; it accepted people's ordinary life, inspired by a new heart, a new spirit, and a new vision, as all that God desired. When religious leaders realize this, then religion can begin to be healthy, and will appeal to people.

So we see Jesus speaking in very down-to-earth parables and stories about life and about His values and His vision of what our life could be. Remember the time Jesus went to Bethany on the occasion of Lazarus' death. When He finally arrived, Martha scolded Him for not coming on time. Jesus tried to calm her down and told her that her brother would rise again. Martha retorted, "I know he will rise again in the resurrection on the last day," indicating that Jesus had talked to them at some time or other about the last things, and about the dead rising to new life, which was not known before Jesus revealed its existence.

The thing that is so astounding is the utter simplicity with which Jesus instituted His New Way. Nothing pompous, no thunderbolts from on high. No secret meetings with chosen ones to deliver dramatic decrees to the waiting, frightened populace. Utter simplicity! Jesus came to share His life with the people. The law, the prophets, the structure, was a scaffold, a preparation for His coming. Now that He had arrived, the prefigures were needed only as reminders, or as hope for those still expecting. The animal sacrifices paled in light of the true Lamb of God's presence in the very shadow of the temple. It was this Lamb that, in God's eyes, gave meaning to all the other sacrifices. After all, how could killing an animal atone for human sin? It was the true Lamb, God's Son, Who gave meaning to all that preceded. "Behold the Lamb of God who takes away the sins of the world," John declared under the Spirit's inspiration.

Jesus had preached His message of hope and freedom and salvation. The Light of the World had radiated the brilliance of God's love to a world that was fast losing hope. He had gathered thousands of His people into a new community, a community in which there would be no vestige of the complex structure of laws and prohibitions and rituals that had so burdened their lives. They were a preparation for His coming, a discipline, and a teaching vehicle. But once He came, He had to achieve a truly cosmic undertaking, nothing less than the rebalancing of the whole spiritual universe that had been disoriented by Adam and Eve's decision to set their human family on a course independent from its Creator. They had lost for their children the blessed gift of intimacy with God that had been such a beautiful part of their original paradise. They had "wounded" God, and neither they nor their children could ever atone for such a monstrous affront. Only a divine being who was also human could offer adequate atonement, and that was to be in His own death which He gladly offered to win back His Father's beloved creation from the power of the evil one.

Setting His people free was part of His main goal. Bringing them back into His Father's family was part of that gift. How Jesus did this was truly a mark of His genius. A simple rite, not painful or bloody, but a mere washing in water, or if that was not feasible, a pouring or a sprinkling of water, as the late-first century Christians testify to in the ancient document, the *Didache,* the Teaching of the Twelve Apostles. Through this simple rite with the corresponding commitment to Himself as Savior, Jesus, in some beautiful mystical yet real way channeled God's life into the believing soul, bringing that child of Adam and Eve back into God's family, to share His life forever in His Kingdom. St. Peter refers to this baptism as a rebirth, in which the newly baptized become partakers of the very divine life of God Himself, which lifts us from the level of mere creatures to the status of children of God, with rights as heirs of a Father who is King and Lord, of the whole universe.

Jesus realized this life He was sharing was fragile and easily shattered or smothered, so He gave His apostles the authority to reconcile those who had drifted or severely damaged their friendship with God, and to anoint and heal those who were sick and troubled in body and soul. He also gave His disciples a food which, if they partook of it, would nourish the divine life within them and deepen their intimacy with Himself. This mystical yet real food was His own "flesh and blood for the life of the world." He also promised His followers that when they accepted His friendship, He and His Father would come and live within them. In this He showed the tenderness that He and His Father felt for weak, crippled human beings. How a God could want to enter into an intimate friendship with such is the mystery of God's love. Jesus came to reveal to us this mystery, but it is too far beyond our ability to comprehend. It is a stupendous honor that God has lifted us up from a state of hopelessness and near despair to a state of wonderment and awe as we contemplate His goodness. We can look at our shabbiness, our poverty, the meanness of our condition, and with tears in our eyes at the wonder of it say to ourselves, "God loves me. I don't know why. I have done nothing to earn it or deserve it, but God loves me. What a wonderful God!"

This gift of God's living within us is the basis for the unique kind of mysticism we see in the lives of many of the saints, and which is open to any who sincerely draw close to God. It is a natural growth of the divine life received in baptism, except in many cases the relationship is not nourished. Unfortunately, rarely do clergymen preach about this mystical life we can have with God and how we can prepare ourselves for it. Another rich source of information about this intimacy with God is the lives of the saints. We have lost so much inspiration and practical guidance in casting aside the saints. They allowed God's grace to flow freely through their lives and have so much to teach us. They used to be powerful role models for our young people. It is sad we have deprived our children of this rich source of inspiration, which they have only too readily replaced with sports heroes of dubious sanctity.

This intimacy with God was the source of Jesus' own strength in His humanity. It flowed from the rich prayer life that He nourished constantly. That is the secret to intimacy with God—constancy in prayer, because it develops within the soul a communion and a sharing of thoughts and feelings between the soul and God, which, over a period of time, can change a person's whole life. It is this kind of prayer that bonds the soul to God and opens it to the flow of God's wisdom and knowledge. This is how we learn about God and about Jesus, and understand their inner life more clearly.

So many times in the Gospels we see Jesus alone. It was so He could draw near to His Father, and draw the strength He needed. However, it happens with such frequency that you begin to wonder if there were other reasons He had this need to be alone. One cannot help but sense that Jesus, as busy as He was each day, felt very much alone. He was not necessarily lonely, but He was alone. This aloneness is striking and opens up an avenue of thought about Jesus that prompts the question, why was He alone? Was He lonely? Did He just like His peace and quiet? Did He feel a need to get away from the crowds?

Jesus was different. Even though He loved the apostles, they certainly could not fill the needs that He had for friendship. Jesus was highly cultured, with a mind as sharp as a laser, and an emotional life that was warm and passionate. His interests were far beyond what anyone could even fathom. The things He thought about and troubled over He could share with no one. Who would understand? His vision reached into the heavens and down to the limits of the netherworld. With whom could He share, who could even begin to understand? So when He was troubled, He needed to be alone, to be with His Father, and, on occasion, with ministering angels.

The apostles, as much as Jesus loved them, were of little solace when He needed comforting. During His most painful crisis, they all fell asleep. When He was with them, their minds were on simple things like what are we going to do for lunch, or if we follow Jesus, how will we earn a living? What will we do with our wives? And our children? Why did He choose this fellow to work with us? I could never stand him; now we are stuck with him for the rest of our lives. So to find peace and quiet, Jesus had to slip away from everyone and be alone. It did not mean that He was lonely, except as loneliness means having no one with whom to share or to return the depth of love one is capable of giving, or not being able to pour out one's heart to another who can truly understand.

Yet Jesus had friends, and though He was God, still entered into wonderfully warm relationships. He felt particularly comfortable with Mary Magdalene, for example. It may be shocking, but she apparently was a passionate woman with a deep capacity for love. There were few who could ever give back to Jesus the love He was able to give as a friend. Mary was one of them. She had so much to give, and a deep friendship between the two was natural. Lazarus and his sisters, Mary and Martha, were others. They were perhaps not as passionate as Mary Magdalene, but warm and comforting and stable, and always there when He needed a friend. They were great for throwing parties, which Jesus loved, parties which well-placed friends from Jerusalem would attend. On these occasions Jesus could discuss His message in a casual, relaxed atmosphere, where even well-intentioned Pharisees could listen without feeling under scrutiny by suspicious colleagues.

CHAPTER 12

PARADISE

WHEN JESUS WENT UP into the hills to be alone and to commune with God, present to Him was the home He had left when He came to earth. His awareness of heaven was not imagined, but real, and on the one occasion when He briefly broke the news of heaven to the apostles, one senses a home-sickness as He tells them, "(If they only knew what my home is like.) The eye has not seen, nor has the ear ever heard, nor has it ever entered into the human imagination what wonderful things my Father has prepared for those who love Him." And then on another occasion, "In my Father's house there are many mansions, and I go to prepare a place for you."

Jesus obviously intended this promise of heaven to be not just something to be shared as a dream, but a powerful moti-vating force in our lives. Life in Jesus' day was bleak and, for so very many, desolate and without meaning. People in His day had no idea of a heaven. Some may have theorized about it, but had no real certainty. Greek and Roman philosophers tried to deduce its existence, but for them it would always be nothing more than a hypothesis. The Jewish people knew of a place of shadows, *Shaol,* but they were not sure what it was, whether it was a real place or just a place in people's memories.

Jesus' announcement that He came down from heaven, His Father's home, was a stunning revelation. If He had taught nothing else, that one promise alone changed our destiny. Only God can promise heaven, and Jesus did. It is not something we can take for granted. It is God's home. The fact that Jesus Himself revealed its existence will always be the most convincing testimony possible. He was not known as a Don Quixote or an impractical dreamer, nor did He have a reputation for spinning tales of the unreal or the untrue. When a person as solid as that says something, intelligent people are compelled to listen and give assent.

Every now and then we hear people remarking that if someone were to come back from the dead and tell them about heaven, they would believe. But would they? Sometimes you hear those words right after a funeral. I could never help but wonder what kind of proof they would need to be convinced. If someone were to come back from the dead and tell them they experienced heaven, would they believe?

I thought and thought about that, and I concluded that even if someone came back from the dead, these people would still not believe. Their questioning minds would soon suggest, "Well, maybe he or she wasn't really dead. Maybe it was just an unusual state of mind, or a psychological state we as yet know nothing about. Maybe it was just a dream the person experienced while in this dreamlike state of suspended animation. It would not take us long to talk ourselves out of this powerful evidence that the person had given to us about heaven. That is why the testimony of Jesus will always be the greatest and most convincing evidence of heaven's existence. The honesty of Jesus, His mental balance as a human, His intellectual caliber, His integrity, and His willingness to die for His message, for the Good News He came to bring us—all these things make Jesus a very credible witness. So when you meet a person of Jesus' reputation saying, "If you are willing to take up your cross and follow me, one day you will live with me in the kingdom of heaven" or that "I am going to prepare a place for you, and I will come and take you with me," you cannot help but believe Him.

What is this heaven Jesus talked about, and which He promised to those who accepted Him? Where is it? One of the cosmonauts radioed back from far out in space and made the cynical remark, "We are so many miles out into space and there is still no sign of heaven." How cynical, how childish to think someone could reach heaven in a spaceship!

What is this heaven like? Is it a place? Is it far away? How do you arrive there? These are questions we would all like to have answered. We know of heaven only from the New Testament. Besides Jesus talking about heaven, St. Paul mentions it, but only briefly. He said on one occasion that he was taken up into heaven, whether in the senses or out of the senses, he could not tell, but he was taken up on one occasion to the seventh heaven, then on another occasion to the third heaven. There must be all the in between heavens. Were these heavens similar to the mansions Jesus talked about?

John the Evangelist, in the Book of Revelation, talks about a vision he had of heaven. It is a real place, unlike anything he had ever seen on earth, indescribably beautiful. There are hills and valleys of a sort, and meadows, but unlike anything on earth. They are magnificent to behold. And there are rivers and streams, but they seem to be composed not of water, but of flowing crystal. And there are beings there, but unlike anything on earth. There is no language to describe them, but they are beautiful beyond description. There are also buildings of a sort, not of crude earth materials, but of substances that seem like precious gems, because light shines through them, a light that comes not from a sun, but a light that emanates from the majesty of God and permeates the whole vast kingdom. You bask perpetually in the warmth of God's love, which flows from this light. That is about all that John could say. But one still tries to visualize and understand what he is attempting to describe. You look at the world around and know it is only a hint of what heaven is like. Your mind naturally begins to analyze.

The sky is blue, a soft, gentle, soothing blue. Thank God it is not black or red all the time. How depressing or maddening that would be. And the clouds that float across the airy blue ocean ever so gracefully; sometimes they are dark and threatening, but mostly they are soft shades of pastel colors. And you look at the sun. It almost blinds you. You begin to realize these things, as beautiful as they are, they are nothing compared to the beauty of heaven.

Or you take a walk through the woods on a warm spring day. You are thrilled by the thousands of wildflowers springing up out of the frozen earth, and caught up in the magic of life emerging from the icy ground. You hear the birds singing in a concert of myriad happy voices. You know God is trying to say something, to deliver some kind of happy message to a soul that needs peace. And you listen carefully and hear the gentle breeze floating through the leaves. It reminds you of the Spirit of God hovering over the waters and over the earth, caressing all of creation, warming those who are cold, and comforting those who are stressed. And all the funny animals make you realize God's playful humor.

Or someday you may be standing on a hillside or in a meadow. The sun is setting, and if you are poetically inclined, you can fall into ecstasy as you drink in the beauty of the setting sun as its vast panorama of colors unfolds before your very eyes, every few seconds changing colors like a vast living kaleidoscope across millions of miles of space. And you realize this, too, is nothing compared to the beauty of God's home. Or you may stand on the shore of the ocean and watch the waves crashing up against the rocks, and sense the power and majesty of the ocean. Or stand on the edge of Niagara Falls and contemplate the awesome sight before you as thousands of tons of waters fall in thunderous explosion upon the rocks beneath.

Every year I used to take my mother and father with me on vacation. It was always a surprise for them. If I tried to prepare them beforehand, they would have all kinds of excuses for not being able to go, so I would just call them up the night before and tell them I was leaving on vacation the next day, and would they like to come. They would never turn down the chance. This one summer, after we were all packed into the car, my father asked where we were going. I told him, ''Grand Canyon.''

''What's that?''

"It's a big hole," I replied, knowing what his reaction would be.

"A big hole. I can't believe I'm going on vacation to see a big hole. If I want to see a big hole, all I have to do is walk up to the sand pit."

"But, Dad, you have never seen a hole like this one."

"A hole is a hole. How far away is this hole?"

"About two thousand miles."

"Two thousand miles," he said, aghast. "I must be losing my mind, traveling two thousand miles to see a hole. Well, we'll at least enjoy the sights along the way and our picnics each day. It doesn't take much to make me happy."

The trip was fun. All our trips were fun. My father probably enjoyed them more than my mom and I.

When we arrived at the canyon, it was late at night, so there were no sneak previews. When I announced that we had to get up at four o'clock in the morning, my dad again balked. "Four o'clock. We just got here. It's almost midnight."

We rose at four, dressed, and walked to the brim of the canyon. It was pitch black. As we stood shivering in the cold morning air, the predawn glow began to light up the sky, casting eerie shadows across the vast empty space before us. As the sun rose, laserlike beams shot across the morning sky. The vast panorama began to unfold before our eyes. You could see huge, massive mountains down in the valley that was one mile deep and five miles across. Thousands of layers of rock lay there like the pages of a ten-billion-year-old book, just waiting to be opened and read, pages that held the secrets of creation and the history of life on our planet.

All the shades of blue, red, green, purple, orange, and yellow. Breathtaking in its vastness. All my father could say was "That's a hole! How could anyone stand on the brink of this canyon, look at that sight, and doubt the existence of an intelligent God."

We looked up into the sky and saw the stars, knowing that some of them were no longer there, though they were shining brightly. They had long since burnt out, perhaps a hundred years ago, but their light is just reaching us at 186,000 miles a second. Never again would we wonder whether heaven is big enough to contain all the people God created.

As breathtaking as these wonders are, you realize they are nothing compared to the beauty and the majesty of heaven. And then finally you think of all the sounds in nature, the sounds of water, the sounds of the birds and the animals, and the mysterious sounds of the night, the sound of water and rustling leaves, and the magical sounds of the human voice. And your mind conjures up concertos and symphonies and whatever kind of music thrills your soul, and you wonder, these are only reminders of what is in store for us in heaven.

You then realize that if you were to gather together all the beautiful sights and sounds and experiences in creation and magnify their beauty to infinity, you would have only a dim idea of the beauty and the glory and the majesty of this place where God lives.

There was once a priest with whom I was stationed. He was a good man, very down to earth. He joined the marines during the Second World War to be with the troops in combat. One morning he was talking about a dream he had had the night before. "I was taken to a place I never imagined existed," he said, "a place so indescribably beautiful, it made my heart pound with joy. The sounds I heard, the beautiful beings I saw, were so breathtaking, I wanted with my whole heart and soul to be in that place." When asked what it was like, all he could say was "The strange thing is I can't even begin to describe it because there is nothing in my whole life's experience similar to what I saw in that dream. There are no words to describe what I saw. All I can say is that compared to what I saw in that dream, the most beautiful things on earth now seem like piles of junk. I just want more than anything else to be in that place. The strange thing is, I was told I am going to be there in a short time. I can't wait."

A few weeks later he died, in good health, at only fifty-four years of age. Was it a dream? Was it a vision God gave him to prepare him for his last days? We will never know, but it makes you think of the words of Jesus; "The eye has not seen, nor has the ear heard, nor has it ever entered into the human imagination the wonderful things my Father has prepared for those who love Him."

However, the greatest joy of heaven is none of all these things. The greatest joy of heaven is the joy of seeing God. The greatest joy for an intelligent being is the joy of being in love. And if two human beings, with all their imperfections, weaknesses, and limitations, can fall so madly in love with each other that they want to spend the rest of their lives together, imagine what it must be like to meet God. If you were to gather all the beautiful angels and human personalities that have ever existed and magnified that beauty to infinity, you would still have only a dim idea of the beauty and majesty of God. So at the moment you close your eyes for the last time, and find yourself face-to-face with God in all His radiant glory, that has to be ultimate joy. God looks at you and you behold a love of infinite tenderness and understanding. Then God calls you by name and says "Welcome home!" You look at Him and know in that instant that you have been loved with a love that is beyond your wildest dreams, and then in ecstasy fall so madly in love with God that nothing could ever distract you from that love. That has to be the greatest joy of heaven, the joy of meeting God.

As we think about heaven, we cannot help but wonder where heaven is. We know that heaven is where God is, and God is everywhere. Heaven, then, must be everywhere, all around us, but in a dimension outside the grasp of our senses. It has to be a place no farther away than a thin veil, and so close that if you could reach out into that dimension, you could touch your loved ones whom God has taken home.

This closeness is the basis for the bond that still exists between ourselves and our loved ones who have left us. While they were here on earth, their souls were locked in their bodies and could function ordinarily only through their five senses. When a person dies, it is like a chick breaking out of a shell, or a child being born into a new world. It is frightening. What they had known, though dark and empty, was secure. The new world is frightening. When the child emerges, the light is at first blinding but soon disappears as a world full of wonder unfolds.

When a soul is freed from the body, it becomes like an angel. Angels have no bodies so they cannot know physical presence. But their presence is much more profound and intimate than physical presence. It is so intimate, they know one another's thoughts and feelings. When a loved one dies and is freed from the body, as a spirit that person is closer to family and friends than ever before, so close they know their thoughts and their feelings and can help them in ways that were impossible on earth. Spirits enjoy the same closeness the angels have to one another. In their own subtle ways they can communicate. The night after my father's funeral, my mother was sitting at the kitchen table, thinking, when she felt a hand on her shoulder, pressing firmly as if to say, "Be strong, I am nearby, do not be afraid." She turned around to see who was behind her. No one. Then the experience left. The sensation was so vivid, my mother knew it was my father.

If heaven is only in another dimension, and if loved ones do not change just because they have passed on to the other side, then their love and concern for us still has to be very much a part of their life. They are still close to us, and you can be sure they are going to be responsive to our needs, just as they were before they left. Heaven is not a great mystery in many ways; it is a logical extension of the way we have lived here on earth, and when the time comes, we should not be afraid to approach that beautiful meeting with God.

Will God be critical when we arrive there? No more critical than people saw Jesus when He was on earth. No one was afraid of Him. Sinners flocked to Him because they knew He loved them and understood them, with their well-intended but feeble efforts to be better, stumbling all along the way through life. He saw their goodness through their sins, and could honestly remark, "Her sins, as many as they may be, are forgiven because she loves much." The only ones Jesus had a difficult time with were those who set themselves up as the righteous ones and looked upon others as sinners. Even those people never tired of trying to reach.

Again, in the only example Jesus gave of the Last Judgment, He did not use the Commandments as the basis for the judgment, but how we treat others. "Come, blessed of my Father, into the kingdom prepared for you from the beginning of time;

when I was hungry, you gave me food. When I was thirsty, you gave me drink. When I was naked, you clothed me, and so on.''

And the blessed will ask, ''When, Lord, did we ever see you in these straits?''

And the Lord will reply, ''As long as you did it for the least of my brothers and sisters, you did it for me.''

There are also some souls who arrive at the other side badly bruised and torn. Some persons have such a sensitive nature, they find life unbearably difficult. They try hard, much harder than others, to cope with life, but find their encounter with others and the normal challenges of life excruciating. They are like a person hanging on for dear life at the end of a rope. They hang on as long as their inner strength holds out. Then, from exhaustion, their fingers slip and they fall . . . mercifully into the loving arms of a loving God. A saintly man once told me that in a vision he had of heaven, he saw Jesus walking through heaven, comforting and healing people who had arrived there still troubled and hurting. On earth Jesus tried to help people understand that God knows our weakness and our efforts. He understands our struggling, our pain, our determination to do better. As long as we are sensitive to the pain and loneliness of others, and reach out to heal, our own sins, as many as they may be, will be forgiven.

When we reach that last hour, it should be with expectancy and joyful longing to meet the only One Who truly knows and understands us.

Once we arrive there, will it be boring? Will we be sitting around playing harps? God forbid, unless we like playing harps. I love the sound of harp music, but I have no desire to play one. All those good things that are so natural to us now will find perfect fulfillment in heaven. The cravings of the human soul for learning and art, for music and love and adventure, and for ever-new friendships know no limits. Living a life of love, in a place where all the deepest needs of the human intelligence and the human heart are fulfilled, can never be boring.

CHAPTER 13

THAT OTHER PLACE

JESUS ALSO TALKED ABOUT hell, a subject whose very nature strikes fear into our hearts. Many Christians have been brought up to be more concerned about avoiding hell than focusing their lives on drawing close to God. As understanding as Jesus was, He still had to face the fact that some people may choose not to love God and to live a life of selfishness. Jesus told some rather gruesome parables about these kinds of people. "There was a rich man named Dives (which means "rich man"), and a poor leper named Lazarus (which means "leper"). Dives lived in a mansion and feasted sumptuously every day. Lazarus sat outside at the gate of the rich man's house, hoping someone might throw him some scraps from the rich man's table, but it never happened. In fact, dogs used to come and lick Lazarus' sores.

One day, Lazarus died. He went straight to heaven. Soon

after, Dives died. He went straight to hell. When he looked up and saw Lazarus in heaven, having a good time, he wished Lazarus would just dip his finger in some water and let a few drops fall upon his parched and burning tongue. But it could never be. He asked Abraham if he might go back and warn his brothers, because they were heading for the same place. Abraham told him that it would do no good. "They have Moses and the prophets to warn them. If they do not listen to Moses or the prophets, they would not listen even if someone were to come back from the dead."

Jesus also told about the fate of the selfish at the Last Judgment. "Depart from me, you accursed, into the everlasting fires prepared for the devil and his angels. When I was hungry, you gave me no food. When I was thirsty, you gave me no drink. When I was naked, you did not clothe me. . . ."

" 'When, Lord, did we ever see you in such need?' they will ask.

"And the Lord will answer, 'As long as you refused to do it to the least of my brothers and sisters, you refused to do it to me.' "

God may seem unreasonably cruel. The truth is, we do not know just how God will ultimately dispose of people who have chosen to do evil things. God's justice is not like human justice which judges only by superficial and circumstantial evidence. God's justice sees deeply into the human heart and understands every detail of what has molded and inspired our lives and led us to making the decisions we make and to leading the kind of lives we live. People may like to judge who is truly evil and have the morbid satisfaction of knowing who is going to hell, but we have to leave that judgment up to God. It is interesting that nowhere did Jesus ever declare any particular human being to have gone to hell. He never even specified that Judas went to hell. All He said was that "it would have been better if he had never been born." I know a lot of people about whom the same thing could be said, but that does not mean that they are going to hell.

However, the existence of hell does seem to be a logical deduction. If a person spends his or her life centered around God and is truly concerned for others, that person wil die with those same attitudes. After death, they will still be centered around God and concerncd for others. It is logical that their life after death will still be centered around God, and among good people.

If a person chooses to live a life centered around self and has consciously decided that he or she does not want to have anything to do with God or with human beings in anguish, life after death will just be a logical extension of the way the person chose to live his or her whole existence. It would be logical for the person to find an existence after death living together with others who are totally self-centered and unconcerned about others. God cannot force people to love Him. If they choose not to love Him, how can He force them to live with Him forever? It does not make sense.

Whether God has condemned any human beings to hell, we have no way of knowing. That's God's business. All we know is that Jesus did say the place exists for the devil and his angels and that he warned mean and totally selfish people that that is a possibility for them if they do not change their ways.

CHAPTER 14

UNFINISHED BUSINESS

As Jesus' days on earth were drawing to a close, we catch a glimpse of His remarkable serenity and courage in the face of imminent doom. He could see where events were leading and continued to carry on His Father's work right to the end. He knew He would not leave this earth until it was all accomplished. Nothing or no one could alter that. So He set His mind firmly on what lay ahead. There was, for example, the approaching Passover, which was laden with figures and symbols and which He would identify with His own Immolation, as the only Sacrifice that could realistically atone for the evils of humanity. There were messages to be delivered to the leaders of the people. There was unfinished business with the apostles. They were still not certain of even who He was. Peter proclaimed Him as the Messiah, the Christ, the Son of the Living God. How much he understood of what he had uttered under divine inspiration we do not know. The other apostles knew even less. It was hard for the Jewish mind to conceive of a man walking down the street as being the awesome God of Sinai. One day Jesus brought Peter, James, and John up a very high mountain, and while Jesus had gone off to pray, Moses and Elias appeared to Him and began discussing fateful events about to occur. When the three apostles turned and saw the vision, they were overwhelmed. Just imagine, Moses and Elias talking to Jesus. He really must be important, maybe He is the Messiah. Whatever passed through their minds, they were impressed, and wanted to construct a shrine to commemorate the event. At least these three now saw Jesus in a new light, a light that would stay with them and give meaning to the fearsome events that were to devastate them all. They now knew that whatever happened, it was all tied up in a mystery that Yahweh had planned for their Master. Even though it was beyond their comprehension, something important was taking place in Jesus' life, and in their lives as well. They felt a strange sense of destiny.

Jesus talked about many things during those last few weeks. The Kingdom of God on earth was an urgent concern. He spoke not only to the apostles but to the disciples about the kingdom and how He saw the kingdom. It was like a field of wheat into which an enemy secretly planted weeds to destroy the crop. It was also like a landowner who went out early in the morning to hire workers for his vineyard, guaranteeing them a certain wage. At later times during the day he went out and hired other workers. At the end of the day, he ordered his overseer to pay them all the same wage, which caused consternation among those who endured the heat of the whole day. In this Jesus hints at things that will happen in His Kingdom after He leaves.

He also compares the Kingdom of heaven on earth to a merchant in search of fine pearls. When he finds one really valuable pearl, he sells all that he has to purchase that pearl. The Kingdom of heaven is like a treasure hidden in a field. Again a man sells all that he has to buy that field.

In these examples, Jesus shows the priceless value of the Kingdom, so precious that a person should be willing to sacrifice everything in order to possess it. He is also brutally realistic in warning His followers that the Kingdom of heaven on earth is a family of spiritually weak, crippled people who need redemption, so don't expect it to be the perfect society. He compares the Kingdom of heaven to a fisherman who went out fishing. When he finished, he hauled the net ashore and began sorting the fish. Some were good, others stank to high heaven. So, also, the kingdom on earth, the Church. Again, the Kingdom of heaven is like a man who went out in a boat to drag the bottom of the lake. He dragged in all kinds of things. Some were good, which he could either use or sell. Others were nothing but junk to be thrown away. This was Jesus' way of preparing the apostles and the rest of us from then on to value His kingdom on earth as the greatest treasure He could give us, but that it will always be filled with sinners exhibiting all kinds of offensive behavior. Do not expect the kingdom to be filled with all nice people. It will never be, neither at the top or at the bottom or at any other level. If it is doing its job, it will be filled with sinners. When sinners are no longer welcome and are excluded, it ceases to be the church of the Good Shepherd. So stay focused on the treasure you have been given, and when you see bad things happening in the kingdom, do not give in to disillusionment and walk away to embrace a fantasy that has no substance. Too many have done this throughout history.

Jesus was also concerned about certain attitudes among the apostles. When the group was passing through Samaria on the way to Jerusalem, the Samaritans were hurt and angry because Jesus was on His way to Jerusalem. They refused to welcome Him to their village. James and John were indignant and asked Jesus if they should not call down fire and brimstone from heaven to destroy them. It bothered Jesus that after being with them for all this time, they still did not absorb His spirit. He nicknamed the two brothers right on the spot the "Sons of Thunder" because of their vindictiveness.

One day Peter came up to Jesus and asked, "Lord, how often should I forgive one who offends me? Seven times?" To which Jesus responded, "No, Peter, not seven times, seventy times seven times. As often as someone offends you, forgive." The conversation comes to an abrupt end as Peter walks away scratching his head. "Seventy times seven, that's a lot of times. I thought I was being bighearted in forgiving seven times. It's still a lot. It doesn't seem possible, seventy times seven times."

So many have had a problem with those words of Jesus, yet He said them and obviously intended they be taken seriously. What did He mean? Was it just a way of speaking? Or did He mean just what He said?

On the surface, it is so unlike Jesus to place such a difficult psychological burden on people. He had come to lift the burdens from people's hearts. It doesn't make sense that He should lay this kind of a burden upon His followers. What was His purpose?

All my life I pondered over that injunction of Jesus to forgive endlessly. In meditating on His life, it was clear He practiced what He preached. He always forgave, though it might not have seemed obvious. When you think of Who He was and the way people treated Him considering Who He was, you might think He would have been highly insulted. He went to Nazareth, His hometown. The very people He lived with for thirty years turned against Him and tried to kill Him in a moment of rage. He slipped through their midst and left town. He showed no rancor. He spent practically His whole public life in and around Capharnaum, performing countless miracles, yet the people there as a whole did not embrace Him or His message and turn to God. The same with Bethsaida. It hurt Him that they were so unreceptive, and He lamented over their fate, which He foresaw in a vision of the future when Roman legions would destroy them. His beloved Jerusalem, which broke His Heart as it had broken the Heart of His Father through the ages past. Again He wept when He saw what would eventually befall the city.

He would preach His message to the people one day. They liked what He had to say, but it was too dreamy. He was a nice man, but He was a dreamer. His message was too simple, too idealistic. They really wanted a military man, a powerful general as Messiah. Jesus was a disappointment, so they wandered away. The next day they would come back, not to hear His message, but to bring their sick, their crippled, their blind, and their tortured for Him to heal. Ignoring their rejection of His message, He would again reach out without the slightest trace of bitterness to heal and comfort and calm their troubled in spirit.

Even with the scribes and Pharisees who hounded His every step, He tried over and over again to break down their self-righteous shell that cut them off from God's mercy. When they invited Him to their homes for dinner, He always accepted. They did not treat Him nicely or extend to Him the ordinary marks of courtesy, but He was always gracious.

It is interesting that with all the good that Jesus did for people, there is only one example of a person coming back to thank Him, and he was a foreigner. And finally His enemies arrested Him and turned Him over for crucifixion. As He hung naked on the cross, looking down upon His executioners, all He could think to say was "Father, forgive them; they know not what they do."

Jesus did practice what He preached about forgiveness, but it still does not explain the reason He insisted on such absolute forgiveness. Most people have compromised over the injunction, deciding, "Well, I'll forgive, but I will never talk to that person again." That is not forgiveness. It is a very satisfying form of vengeance, especially if it is toward a parent or a brother or sister, or one you have loved deeply. It is a refusal to ever again show love to that person. It is cutting that person off from all the important things in your life. It is telling that person that you really do not care to know what happens to them, whether good or tragic. If the person dies, well, you will probably find out about it, and utter a pious prayer to satisfy your obligation to love. Then the relationship is finally ended. That is a most horrible kind of meanness. And it is always justified in such a carefully thought out, self-righteous way. I read a book recently in which two brothers had not talked to each other for years. While their mother was dying, she was being cared for at the home of one of the brothers. He never told his brother that their mother was dying. The mother died and he still refused to tell him. The brother found out too late, to his unbearable grief, that his mother had died. The name of the book is *Blood Brothers* by Elias Chacour. It is a beautiful story about forgiveness in a family of Palestinian Arab Christians whose ancestors had lived in the Holy Land since the time of Jesus, and were driven from their homes, which were then dynamited.

That was the kind of hatred and meanness that Jesus witnessed time and again. There was a law in effect that sanctioned such behavior; "An eye for an eye and a tooth for a tooth." If someone injured you, you could inflict a comparable injury on that person. Its implications are frightening.

Jesus brought up that issue one day. "It used to be said, 'An eye for an eye and a tooth for a tooth,' but I say to you, unless you forgive your brother from your heart, neither will your heavenly Father forgive you." It seemed continually on Jesus' mind, as He stresses the same theme on other occasions. It is an essential part of Jesus' message. He did, after all, come to reconcile the world to His Father's love, to obtain His forgiveness for the sins of His human family, and to insist that His followers learn to rise above pettiness and hurt and also forgive.

One day, only a few years ago, it dawned on me what Jesus was trying to teach. And I then realized He was not imposing an impossible burden on His followers, but was providing the key to true inner peace, and also for peace in the world. "If you want to have peace within yourself, and with your neighbors, learn to forgive." In fact, He is really driving at something much deeper, and something He Himself practiced. Do not even take offense, but try to understand the pain and tortured spirit that gave rise to such persons' offensive behavior. Then, when you see their pain, or their oddness, you pity them, and do not take on the anguish they are trying to pass on to you. It makes such good sense. It is not easy, and Jesus realized it is not easy, but it is the only way to preserve peace and serenity. Once we begin to practice it each day, it does become easier, until eventually it becomes second nature.

CHAPTER 15

PASSION

OCCASIONALLY WE ENCOUNTER A person who knows he has
to face a difficult ordeal, and steadfastly do what has to be
done, even if he loses his life in the process. It is unheard of,
however, that a person entered this world knowing that the
purpose of his life was to die. Jesus' mission was to reconcile
the human race to His heavenly Father, and He would accomplish this by offering His life for the atonement of sin, and in
the process convince people of how precious they were to
God. As those days approached, we see Him becoming more
pensive. It was not easy to decide to die, even though He knew
at the end of it He would be home again with His Father. With
His divine vision, He could see clearly the manner of His
death, and He could not help but shudder at the thought of it.
Still, "He set His face steadfastly towards Jerusalem."

When He arrived there, it was Passover time. The city was

crowded and tense. People who had come from faraway places were looking for Him. He was the Person to watch. Would He declare Himself and announce to the world He was the Christ, the anointed One of God? Would the leaders accept Him? Would there be a revolution? He has all kinds of powers, some of which we have not even seen as yet. And He is fearless. He certainly has what it takes. He obviously is in control of His destiny. He knows just what He is doing, but what is it? What is the purpose of all the remarkable things that He does?

Jesus and the apostles approached Jerusalem from the western side, through Bethphage on top of the Mount of Olives. He sent two disciples to the village ahead to fetch a "tethered donkey and a colt with her." "If anyone says anything, tell them the Master needs them and will send them back at once."

When the animals were brought to Him, there was a sense of mystery. The apostles put their cloaks on the donkey, and Jesus, in imitation of King David, His ancestor, rode down the hillside, across the Kedron Valley, and into the city. People streaming into the city for the feast saw Him coming and gathered along the route to welcome Him, singing with all their hearts, "Hosanna to the Son of David! Blessed is He Who comes in the name of the Lord! Hosanna in the highest heavens!" It had been prophesied by the prophet Zechariah that the Messiah would come "humbly, riding on a donkey."

As He entered the city, He continued on, straight for the temple. The excitement reached fever pitch, as Jesus allowed the chief priests and the political leaders to see that He had the power of the whole population behind Him and could take over the government if He so chose. That, however, was not

His purpose. His kingdom was not of this world. It is a kingdom of the spirit, and as such the temple was very much His concern. It was His Father's house, and they had turned it into a stockyard full of animal filth, so they could become rich on the sale of concessions in His Father's sanctuary. That was intolerable.

He alighted from the donkey and its colt, telling His disciples to return them to the owner, and, picking up a rope, He knotted it and began driving the animals out of the temple, overturning the tables of the money changers. Approaching the dove sellers, the offerings of the poor, He merely says, "Get these things out of here."

The chief priests and politicians were furious but could do nothing. He was in absolute control, and they knew He knew it.

After making His statement, Jesus calmly walked out of the city and went to Bethany, where He spent the night, and the next few nights leading up to the Passover. In the mornings He returned to the city and continued preaching His message boldly. "There was a landowner who planted a vineyard and let it out to tenants and went abroad. At vintage time he sent servants to collect the produce, but the tenants seized the servants, beat one, killed another, and stoned a third (describing various prophets' fates). The owner sent more servants, who were also treated violently. Finally he sent his son, thinking, 'They will certainly respect him.' But when they saw the son coming, they thought, 'This is the heir. Let us kill him and then the vineyard will be ours.' So, taking the son and dragging him *outside the vineyard,* they killed him."

The chief priests knew He was talking about them, and

were furious, and would have arrested Him, but they were afraid of the crowd who loved Him, and looked upon Him as a prophet.

Finally, Passover arrived. Jesus had been longing to celebrate this last feast with the apostles. Thursday evening they gathered at a furnished upstairs room, and, spreading the table, began their sacred feast. As they partook of the symbolic foods and reminisced over events in their people's history, they settled down to a long, enjoyable evening.

Toward the end, however, Jesus became solemn, and spoke in tender, sentimental language, explaining to the apostles His love for them and His concern for their future. He knew them only too well, and as He told them He was leaving, which they could in no way understand, He prayed that they would always be one in His love, and that there would always be unity in His family.

As His words begin to penetrate, and they showed their sadness, He promised to be with them always. At the end of the meal He took a loaf of unleavened bread, broke it, and passed it to them with the words "Take this and eat it. This is My Body which will be given up for you." Then He took a cup of wine and passed it to them, saying, "Take this, all of you, and drink from it. This is the cup of My Blood, the Blood of the new and eternal covenant, which will be shed for you and for the many for the forgiveness of sins. Do this in my memory." In some beautiful, mystical way, Jesus fulfilled the promise He had made months before to give His Flesh and Blood as the food of their souls. In doing this, He created an intimate way of being with His friends long after He had left them, a new and comforting kind of presence that would bring joy and a sense of intimacy to those who would believe His words for many centuries to come.

After the meal they walked out of the city, across the valley to the Mount of Olives, where they frequently spent the night. On this night, however, Jesus knew it was His last, and needed to be with His Father. What went through His mind that night we could never comprehend. As a person with divine intelligence, He could see and feel the whole drama unfolding as vividly as if it were taking place then and there. He could feel the emotions and the pain. The crisis for Jesus involved His responsibility to make the decision to undergo the trial and torture. In His divine will He already made His decision. If, however, He was to represent humanity in offering the sacrifice of Himself, He had to choose it as a human as well. That was the crisis. Seeing so vividly what it entailed and feeling the pain and torture so keenly, it made His whole being shudder with a feeling of revulsion and terror, which was so intense, it forced blood to ooze through the blood vessels and come out through the pores of His skin. The Gospel writers described the phenomenon, which they did not understand, as Jesus sweating blood.

In this crisis Jesus pleaded, "Father, if it is possible, let this chalice pass from me. Yet, not my will, but your will be done."

During this agony, the apostles were of little comfort. They had all fallen asleep.

All during the trial, Jesus showed nothing but calm and perfect composure. Even before the Roman governor He was calm, giving the impression that even under these circumstances, He controlled the situation. "Does it not trouble you," Pilate asked, mystified at His composure, "that I have power of life and death over you?" Jesus' response puzzled the governor even more. "You would have no power over me had it not been given to you from above."

Although Pilate knew he had no reason to convict Jesus, He found Him guilty and condemned Him to death by crucifixion. Jesus was taken, dragged outside the walls of Jerusalem, fulfilling His prophecy about the wicked tenants of the vineyard, and crucified.

At the foot of the Cross was His mother, John, and Mary Magdalene. At a little distance were a few faithful friends. The other apostles were nowhere to be seen.

After asking His Father to forgive His enemies, and promising paradise to the repentant thief on the Cross next to Him, and instructing John, the beloved disciple, to care for His mother as if she were his own, He looked up to heaven, breathing His last words. "It is finished. Father, into your hands I send my Spirit." And He died, at the moment He chose.

The centurion who pierced His heart with a lance was profoundly touched by Jesus' death, and after remarking, "This man truly was the Son of God," spent the rest of his life in Jesus' footsteps.

A wealthy member of the Jewish ruling body, Joseph of Arimathaea, and a secret follower of Jesus', took Jesus' body from the Cross, placed it in His mother's arms for one last embrace, then with respect buried it in his own tomb, which was nearby. The tomb was then sealed by the governor's orders, a guard was placed to secure it, and the family and friends left. It was Passover.

CHAPTER 16

NEW LIFE AND NEW HOPE

FOR THREE DAYS THERE was nothing but a quiet, restless peace over the city. The word of Jesus' death had spread throughout the capital, casting a pall over the great feast. It was hard to believe how a man who had done nothing but heal and comfort and console, who had spent His whole life doing good and preaching peace and forgiveness and love of one another, even enemies, could have been treated so cruelly and brutally. How could it have happened? What is happening to us? And there were no answers except that evil can never tolerate the presence of goodness, least of all Goodness Himself.

On the third day, news began to spread. Three women, hoping to anoint Jesus' body, went to the tomb early Sunday morning. The tomb was empty; the soldiers had gone. But two strange persons, brilliant in appearance but not quite human, were present at the tomb, and told them that He had risen as He had promised.

The women returned to tell the apostles, who were in hiding, that Jesus had risen. They laughed at the women, calling it women's fantasy. But Peter and John did go to the tomb and found it empty, with no trace of Jesus. They returned to their hiding place more depressed than ever. For the rest of the day there was no further news.

Then, late in the afternoon, two disciples were walking home to Emmaus, a sabbath day's journey west of Jerusalem. On the way they met a stranger, who joined them on the journey. They talked along the way about Jesus and their dashed hopes. The stranger reminisced about the prophecies concerning the Messiah, trying to help them understand. When they reached Emmaus, the stranger accepted their invitation to stay with them. As they were eating supper, they watched the stranger breaking bread, and in realizing it was Jesus, He disappeared.

I always thought there was a lot of humor in what happened next. Jesus knew the disciples would run as fast as they could back to Jerusalem to tell the apostles. But after not approaching the apostles all day long, now, all of a sudden, He has to reach them before the two disciples. It seems He was having fun with this new kind of glorified body that could move with the speed of thought.

Arriving at the apostles' hiding place, he could have gently rapped at the door and quietly called to them, "It's me, let me in!" They would have been shocked but pleasantly surprised. Not Jesus. He was not beyond having fun with the apostles, like the time they saw Him walking on the lake in the middle of the night as they were being tossed about by the violent storm. Now, rather than make an ordinary entrance, He has to make a dramatic appearance. It is night. The room is dark and smoky from the oil lamps, which are casting strange shadows around the room. Suddenly, Jesus passes through the solid walls and appears in their midst. They are absolutely terrified, and jump to their feet, aghast, speechless.

"Well, don't just stand there. It's me."

They did not know how to respond, thinking it was a ghost.

"It is me. I will show you. Give me a piece of fish. A ghost cannot eat a piece of fish."

They offered Him a piece of fish, which He ate. Then they all sat down and tried to relax.

"Be at peace," Jesus said to them. "Receive the Holy Spirit, whose sins you shall forgive, they are forgiven them. Whose sins you shall retain, they are retained."

After spending some time with them, Jesus left. Not long afterward the two disciples arrived, breathless, banging at the door, eager to share the good news. Imagine their surprise when the apostles told them, "Oh, we know He's alive. He just left." The incident, I think, shows the playfulness in Jesus. There has always been humor in God. We just have to look for it between the lines. God is subtle, so is God's humor.

After those beautiful days in which the family was reunited for a time, Jesus' presence and the Spirit He sent to confirm them followed them everywhere they went, throughout Palestine, Asia Minor, India, Africa, Spain, the far reaches of the Roman Empire, bringing to the hurting, troubled, and searching souls the gentle message of this simple Man who happened to be God.